D1693129

Great Debates

by

Luan Hanratty

First edition published in 2012
© Copyright 2012
Luan Hanratty

The right of Luan Hanratty to be identified as the author of this work has been asserted by him in accordance with the Copyright, Designs and Patents Act 1998.

All rights reserved. No reproduction, copy or transmission of this publication may be made without express prior written permission. No paragraph of this publication may be reproduced, copied or transmitted except with express prior written permission or in accordance with the provisions of the Copyright Act 1956 (as amended). Any person who commits any unauthorised act in relation to this publication may be liable to criminal prosecution and civil claims for damage. Although every effort has been made to ensure the accuracy of the information contained in this book, as of the date of publication, nothing herein should be construed as giving advice. The opinions expressed herein are not those of the author.

Cover design by Luan Hanratty

www.teflideas.com

This course from TEFL Ideas comprises twenty-four 2-hour classes incorporating rhetorical, logical, and practical debating techniques and activities. The lessons are specifically aimed at Upper-Intermediate to Advanced level learners but are also perfectly suitable for native-speaking high school students. *Great Debates* is a practical and classical tool for the English language communicators of tomorrow.

Rhetoric

Rhetoric, the art of intelligent communication, is a skill which is not much taught in this day and age. There is a strong movement in ESL instruction that emphasizes using as little stylistic language as possible. This is done to make things easier on learners and it promotes an almost sterile strain of English; mutually comprehensible between second language users internationally. The problem with this is that English is not just spoken in labs and classrooms, post offices and railways stations.

Rhetoric is not just used in poetry and literature either. Almost every aspect of human life and thought depends on the articulation and communication of meaning and thus involves elements of rhetoric. The use of rhetoric in the real world is unavoidable. It is fundamental in communicating meaning and central to language itself. Native speakers use rhetorical devices of some description all the time, without even knowing it. We use rhetoric when we find something that matters to us, something that we feel strongly about and want to take a stand on. It gives us individuality and displays that to others.

Facts and knowledge are needed to communicate well but more importantly, effective communicators do so by presenting things in context. This appeals to the right side of the brain; the emotional and artistic hemisphere of the brain.

If our students wish to be able to communicate to really effectively in English, learning a few rhetorical devices is going to stand them in very good stead for the rest of their English language lives. As well as this, mastery of the tools of rhetoric will allow them to communicate better and more persuasively in their native language too.

Logical Fallacies

The Logical Fallacy is a rhetorical device which has no grounding in actual fact and is used by people to unfairly gain the upper hand in debates. Being unaware of logical fallacies makes us vulnerable to skilled communicators. But, being able spot flaws and spuriousness goes a long way in quashing someone's argument.

Debate

Debating is useful for language learners because it is both formal and interactive. It is also intellectually healthy for people to practice persuasive and logical argument. The arguments contained within this course are written with the aim of creating sophisticated English language thinkers who are able to argue a point from both sides.

The mark of an educated mind is being able to entertain a thought without accepting it.

Aristotle

Lesson Structure

Preamble

The introductory sections contain general information on the subject as well a commentary on a relevant work of art. This is to be read by the teacher and then relayed to the students and simplified where necessary. Some stock debating phrases are included to be modelled and, hopefully, applied in the argument.

Set up and Argument

After discussing the Preamble, take a show of hands on agreement or disagreement with the proposition. Don't allow a lot of abstentions – gently prompt the apathetic students to 'aye' or 'no' one way or the other. Then split the class into two teams and to prepare an argument. By doing this you are making the students play devil's advocate. Alternatively, if there is an even split of opinion in the room you can just allow the students to move to the side of the room they agree with and create a parliamentary-style debating chamber. Using all the space you have and giving the teams enough time are the keys to success here.

The bullet-pointed mini-arguments are for the teacher to help each side during their preparations. Print and cut up these paragraphs so you can distribute one to each person. But make sure that they don't just simply read the slips out verbatim. They must state the point in their own words and expand the points, parry objections etc. They are included as a starting point to give clues to each member so they can make further notes and develop their attacks. Teacher scaffolding and dictionaries are useful here.

After at least ten minutes, ask each team to nominate their captain, who will set out the opening proposal. The opposing team captain has to counter this proposal. Let the teams take turns to put forward their ideas but only allow one person to speak at a time. If you have a large amount of lower levels students in the class, it is good to reverse the order so the 'weaker' students get to speak first and outline some basic arguments, leaving the more complex points to the higher levels during the second half of the debate.

The person who is speaking should be standing to adhere to a sense of oratory in the room, creating more of an impact on the listeners. Any attempts at using rhetoric, e.g. exaggeration, display or bombast, should be highly praised. Any logical fallacies that crop up should be turned over to the opposing team to be torn apart.

The Vote

Take the final vote by call – this is the way it is usually done in Parliament. If it is too close to call, take a show of hands. If that is still too close, you can organize a proper ballot. Either way, it's usually interesting to see how much of a swing in opinion has taken place since all the arguments have been tabled.

Activity

These mostly community-based or real world tasks are to be performed if you have any time remaining.

Vocab Refresh

A list of the key terminology for the class.

Acknowledgements

The questions which shape the debates and inspired the course are adapted from a fantastic website called politicalcompass.org which includes a test for determining political orientation. In order to demonstrate logical fallacies and rhetorical tropes, a few websites in particular were extremely helpful. These were don-lindsay-archive.org, nizkor.org, infidels.org, rhetoric.byu.edu and grammar.about.com.

Many of the functional debating phrases are taken directly from Prime Minister's Questions, which is perhaps the most dynamic and accessible forum for debating in the world. Wikipedia was an invaluable resource providing the basis for comprehensive summaries and some key points to consider. Other helpful resources included the BBC and other news websites, as well as countless blogs and forums of which it is hard for me to credit each and every one. Because of the nature of the internet, content gets proliferated and disappears so much so that it's often difficult to go back and find the original inspiration for some of the ideas. But I have credited them where I can. With this huge wealth of internet information and opinions I was able to go deep on each topic and shape the arguments with pithy and pungent points.

I hope you find *Great Debates* to be both entertaining and educational. It took several years to put together and I believe it should be utilized as a centerpiece in any good curriculum.

Contents List

1.	Sanctions	1
2.	Violence	14
3.	Nature or Nurture	17
4.	Gun Control	42
5.	Distribution of Wealth	55
6.	Healthcare	68
7.	Globalization	82
8.	Drugs	94
9.	Tax	107
10.	Friends & Enemies	120
11.	Contribution to Society	133
12.	Free Trade	145
13.	Reciprocity	158
14.	Civil Liberties	172
15.	Capital Punishment	185
16.	Crime & Punishment	198
17.	Commerce & Culture	211
18.	Adoption	224
19.	Social Order	237
20.	Military Interventionism	250
21.	Free Market	265
22.	Private Healthcare	279
23.	Balancing the Budget	293
24.	Cultural Relativism	306

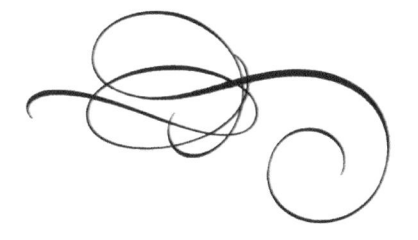

Debate 1 – Sanctions

Debate 1 – Sanctions

Are economic sanctions a useful tool to deal with problem countries?

Goals of the Lesson

- For students to become more familiar with the concept and ethical basis of sanctions.
- For students to practice debating, using persuasive devices and functional phrases.
- For students to find some form of consensus on the issue.

Rhetoric

Discuss and demonstrate these figures of speech with the class and explain that people who are able to speak forcefully and persuasively often use devices like this. Tell the students that you would like them to try and use these devices during the debate.

1. **Anacoenosis** – posing a question to an audience, often with the implication that it shares a common interest with the speaker.

'Now I ask you to decide: Given the persecution my client has undergone, does he not deserve to have some justifiable anger?' ~ Gideon Burton, *The Forest of Rhetoric*

2. **Anacoluthon** – a change in the syntax within a sentence.

'The great white shark — what a fierce animal that is!'

3. **Anadiplosis** – repetition of a word at the end of a clause at the beginning of another.

'Fear leads to anger. Anger leads to hate. Hate leads to suffering.' ~ Yoda, *Star Wars*

Logical Fallacies

The Logical Fallacy is a rhetorical device which has no grounding in actual fact and is used by people to unfairly gain the upper hand in debates. Being able to spot such a flaw goes a long way to invalidating an opponent's argument.

1. **Appeal to Anonymous Authority.**

'Top boffins suggest that …'

'Experts agree that …'

2. **Appeal to Authority.**

'If the doctor says you should take the medicine, then you must do it.'

'The brilliant William Jenkins, the recent Nobel Prize winner in physics, states uncategorically that the flu virus will be controlled in essentially all of its forms by the year 2,050. The opinion of such a great man cannot be disregarded.'

3. **Appeal to Coincidence** – asserting that some fact is due to chance.

'It said this would happen in my horoscope this morning.'

'I know I've missed my last eight penalties, but I've just been really unlucky.'

Preamble

Sanctions are a punishment used as a way of making countries co-operate with the international community. These might include a ban on trade with that country or excessive import / export quotas / tariffs making trade difficult. They also might include the removal of embassies and diplomatic ties.

Examples

1. The United States and Japan imposed sanctions against India following her nuclear tests in 1998. These were subsequently rescinded by the Bush government.

2. The United States has imposed sanctions on Iran for years as a "state sponsor of terrorism".

3. The United Nations imposed stringent economic sanctions upon Iraq after the first Gulf War. These were maintained partly as an attempt to make the Iraqi government co-operate with the UN weapons inspectors' monitoring of Iraq's weapons and weapons programs. The sanctions were only removed after the invasion in 2003.

4. In 1999 The UN froze all bank accounts of al-Qaeda and Taliban associated individuals.

5. The European Union imposed diplomatic sanctions on Cuba after the latter broke an agreement to cease capital punishment in 2003. Measures included limits on high-level government visits.

6. The boycott of the Olympic Games in LA and Moscow by Russia and the US respectively during the height of the Cold War.

7. Sanctions were imposed during apartheid in South Africa while Nelson Mandela was jailed. Despite this, the UK under Margaret Thatcher's Conservative government were the biggest foreign investor in South Africa during this period. South Africa was not able to partake in any international sporting competitions, although some teams defied the ban.

8. The US has imposed sanctions on Cuba since 1962.

9. During the Napoleonic Wars European nations were forbidden to trade with the UK in attempt to cripple Great Britain.

Debating Phrases

Convincing – from the World Schools Debating Championships (2004)

1. The opposition have made some good points, however, they forgot to think about some very important issues.
2. We hear what the opposition are saying but we do not agree.
3. That's one way to think about it, however …
4. Not to play the devil's advocate, but we will prove to you exactly the opposite.
5. At first sight, the opposition's argument seems fair, but …
6. It is easy enough to make broad generalizations, but in reality it is a very complex issue.

Siege of Sevastopol – Ivan Aivazovsky (1859)

Sevastopol is a strategic harbour on the Crimean Peninsula in modern-day Ukraine. It is an important port for the Russian Black Sea Fleet. The city was blockaded by the British Navy during the Crimean War in an attempt to strangle the Russian Empire of food, arms supplies and communications.

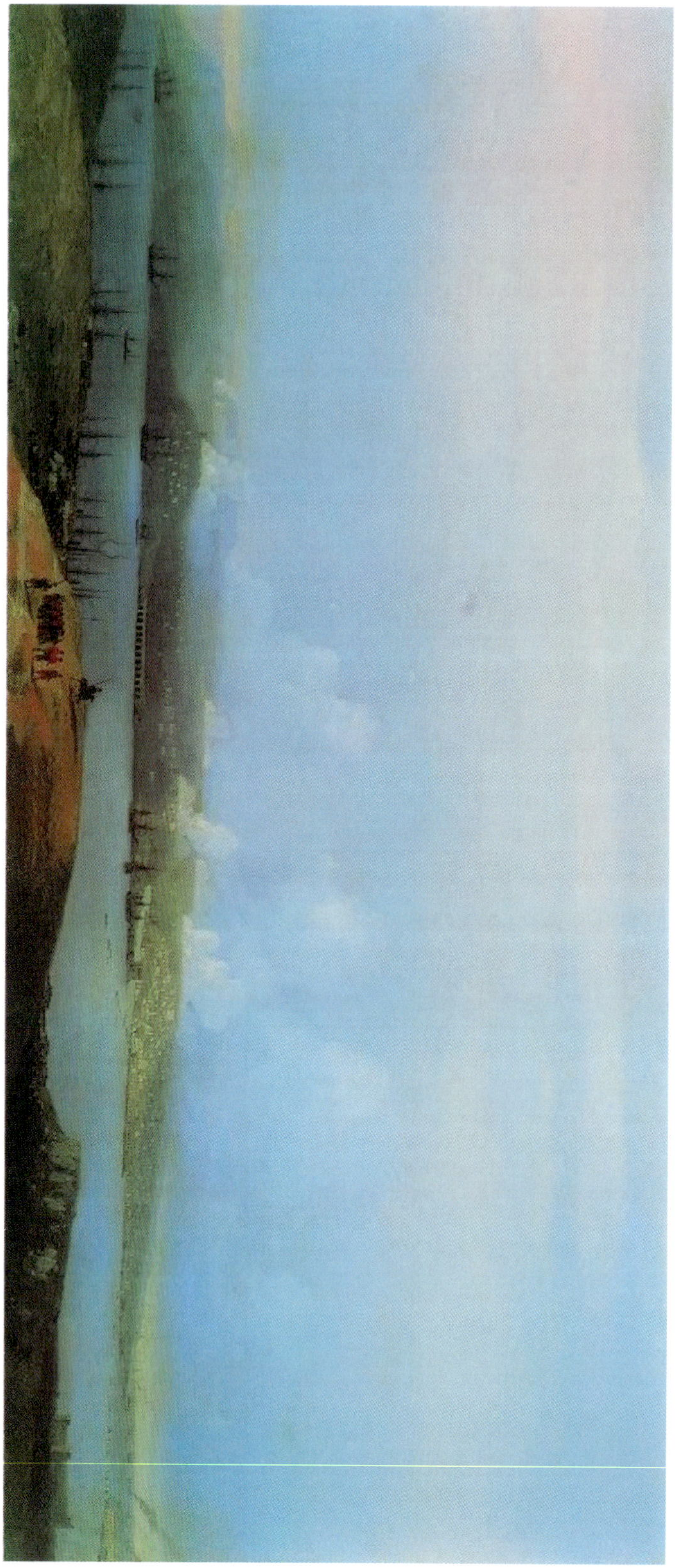

Yes, I'm in favour of sanctions.

- Sanctions isolate a country and are a clear expression of displeasure, signaling to the world what is right and wrong according to the international rule-based system of order. Sanctions build responsible consensus and agreement globally. In an increasingly globalized world, a democratic form of world government in increasingly desirable and possible.

- Sanctions create a difficult internal situation for the country and make it suffer as a result of wrong-doing / bad leadership. They exist for good reason and attempts to get around them are insulting to the victims of the crimes committed by that government / tyrant.

- UN sanctions were the single biggest factor in bringing down the apartheid government in South Africa. Making life uncomfortable for the people will eventually encourage them to remove their leaders. Sanctions therefore, force political change.

- Sanctions are more desirable than war, which is often the only other alternative. Thus sanctions are often the only hope of avoiding war and the last means of diplomacy. Someone famously said that 'war is the ultimate failure of diplomacy' and so sanctions can be seen as a successful outcome that prevents direct conflict.

- Sanctions force people to act, especially when luxury goods are hit. Who consumes the luxuries in poor countries? The powerful… Take for example UN Security Council Resolution 1718 against North Korea in 2006 which banned the sale of: luxury goods, weapons, materials to manufacture weapons, as well as a host of other measures restricting movement and trade. Indeed, these measures quickly forced the DPRK back to the Six-Party talks by targeting strategic interests.

- Sanctions block the import of vital materials and technologies needed to create weapons. These include metals, chemicals, oil, coal, rubber, uranium, etc. Sanctions can prevent terrorism by freezing the bank accounts of groups like al-Qaeda. And even the strictest sanctions allow the import of essentials like food and medicine.

No, I'm against sanctions.

- Sanctions encourage retaliation, which means a vicious cycle of negative measures. Economic sanctions frequently result in trade wars that means increased import tariffs, slower growth and higher unemployment for all. They encourage spiraling one-upmanship.

- Sanctions give up the attempt at dialogue, which has more chance of solving such problems. Diplomatic solutions are always preferable to punishment because they foster agreement. Sanctions are never fully enforceable and thus they are not effective.

- Sanctions on vital products such as food and medicines can seriously harm a society, causing suffering and higher child death rates. The humanitarian toll can be huge. Post-Gulf War sanctions on Iraq – the toughest sanctions in history – clean water, food and basic hospital machines were not available while hospitalized children could not even receive simple toys like teddy bears. Child death rates doubled while literacy rates fell dramatically as fewer children attended school and instead were forced into work. These sanctions did not even succeed in their desired outcome of toppling Saddam.

- Sanctions by the US against Cuba since 1962 have not forced political change. Instead they have frozen out the country and made an almost permanent enemy on her doorstep. Plus, it's always the people who suffer from economic hardship, not the leadership who committed the wrongdoing. Sanctions therefore punish the wrong people.

- Sanctions can backfire and be harmful to the country that imposes them – as in the case of the sanctions against Britain during the Napoleonic Wars, which harmed the economies of many European countries. The 'bad' country can develop into an autarky, which is a self-sufficient economy that does not engage in any international trade.

- Sanctions are often imposed for the wrong reasons. They simply reflect the personal prejudices / disagreements of a particular president and his administration. Sanctions often say more about the government imposing them than they do about the country receiving them.

Great Debates

Legislating a Resolution

This activity is adapted from mismun2012.wikispaces.com.

Now explain that it is time to come to some sort of consensus and conclude the debate. Even though there is most probably disagreement in the room, the losing team must accept defeat gracefully and remember that unity of the state and the rules of the chamber are sacrosanct. The majority have won and thus they can move forward with ratifying a statement to confirm their power and intent. This is important because it puts the information discussed into a framework and establishes the position of the 'country'.

Split the class into groups of four or five and set them the task of writing a closing statement or law. The statement should be <u>one sentence long</u> and contain 3 things:
1. The **name of the organization**, e.g. 'The United Nations Security Counsel / General Assembly', 'European Union', etc.
2. A **preamble part** with a verb that identifies a problem and puts it in context. E.g. 'Having examined…', 'realizing that…', 'understanding that…', 'believing…', 'deciding…'
3. An **operation part** with a verb that proposes or decides on a course of action to be taken, to deal with and solve a problem. E.g. 'expects', 'ensures', 'decides', 'urges', 'condemns', etc.

If students are struggling to make clauses you can hand out the following verbs and examples.

Pre-ambulatory verbs:

Convinced	Having considered	Realizing
Declaring	Having examined	Recognizing
Deeply concerned	Having heard	Seeking
Deeply regretting	Having studied	Taking into account
Fully aware	Noting with approval	Taking note
Believing	Noting with deep concern	Welcoming

Operative verbs:

Accepts	Demands	Recommends
Approves	Emphasizes	Reminds
Calls for	Encourages	Requests
Condemns	Expresses its hope	Strongly condemns
Confirms	Have resolved	Supports
Considers	Notes	Takes note of
Declares	Proclaims	Urges

Body: The UN General Assembly

Pre-ambulatory Clauses:

Noting Article One of the Universal Declaration of Human Rights, which states that 'All beings are born free and equal in dignity and rights',

Aware that economic embargoes cause great damage to nations, both to the individuals within the nations, and to the wider social structure,

Bearing in mind paragraph 70 of the Secretary-General's 1995 report on the work of the United Nations, which stated, "Sanctions raise the ethical question of whether suffering inflicted on vulnerable groups in the target country is a legitimate means of exerting pressure,

Calling the attention of member states to the Vienna Declaration and Programme of action which affirms that food should not be used as a tool for political pressure,

Convinced that it is wrong and immoral for any country to penalize another through prejudice, because they disapprove of their government,

Believing that it is only through building firm trading links, and not through a policy of hatred and intolerance that a lasting peace between nations can be achieved,

Operative Clauses

Calls upon all member states to reconsider their position over all sanctions, and particularly the sanctions on Iraq and Cuba;

Suggests that the sanctions against the above named countries be gradually relaxed, with the aim of reinstating the infrastructure, education system and medical care of both member states;

Expresses its hope that the sanctions will be fully lifted within eight years;

Urges the United Nations to send medical aid to both countries, to alleviate the suffering of the thousands of civilians, especially to pregnant and nursing mothers, and children;

Strongly recommends that the first sanctions to be relaxed on oil in the case of Iraq, and on sugar in the case of Cuba, so that the countries may use the profits from their primary exports to:

(i) invest in the socio-economic structure of their nations, in order to revive their economies,

(ii) provide humanitarian aid, specifically food and medicine, to their population,

(iii) pay teachers and other professionals to return to work, so that the alarming drop-out rate at schools may be remedied, to provide a basic education for the future generation;

Suggests that this process be monitored by the UN and other nations that would be affected, especially those in the Middle East;

Encourages all member states to endeavor to trade fairly with these countries in particular, and troubled regions in general, so that through mutual trade and increased prosperity, lasting peace and friendly relations between countries will ensue.

Vocab Refresh

Quotas / tariffs – regulations on imports / exports designed to limit international trade.

To impose (sanctions) – to force someone to comply with a new law or restriction.

To isolate – to separate from all others.

Tyrant – a dictator or despot. Someone who exercises total control over their nation.

Apartheid – the policy of racial segregation and discrimination practiced in South Africa before 1989.

Diplomacy – is the art of communication between countries.

Vicious cycle – events which reinforce themselves via a feedback loop.

To backfire – when a plan has the opposite effect of what was intended.

Autarky – a self-sufficient country that does not trade with the outside world.

Hardship – suffering; deprivation; oppression.

Prejudices – an immediate often irrational dislike of something or someone.

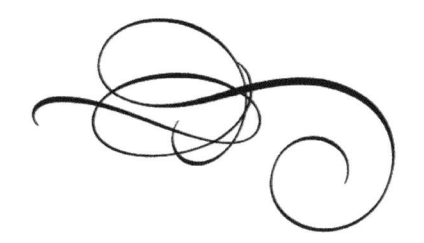

Debate 2 – Violence

Debate 2 – Violence

Who is to blame for increasing youth violence in Western society?

Goals of the Lesson

- For students to become more familiar with the concepts and causes of violence.
- For students to practice debating, using persuasive devices and functional phrases.
- For students to find some form of consensus on the issue.

Rhetoric

Discuss and demonstrate these figures of speech with the class and explain that people who are able to speak forcefully and persuasively often use devices like this. Tell the students that you would like them to try and use these devices during the debate.

1. **Anaphora** – the repetition of the same word or group of words at the beginning of successive clauses.

'*We shall* not flag or fail. *We shall* go on to the end. *We shall fight* in France, *we shall fight* on the seas and oceans, *we shall fight* with growing confidence and growing strength in the air, *we shall* defend our island, whatever the cost may be, *we shall fight on* the beaches, *we shall fight on* the landing grounds, *we shall fight in* the fields and in the streets, *we shall fight in* the hills. *We shall* never surrender.' ~ Winston Churchill

2. **Anastrophe** – inversion of the usual word order. Old English is full of anastrophe to speakers of modern English.

'Right you are.'

'Ready are you? My own counsel will I keep on who is to be trained!' ~ Yoda, *Star Wars*

3. **Antanaclasis** – a form of **pun** in which a word is repeated in two different senses.

'We must all hang together, or assuredly we shall all hang separately.' ~ Benjamin Franklin

'I don't believe that Mr. Bush is a Christian. Christians believe in the prophets, *peace* be upon them. Bush believes in profits and how to get a *piece* of them.' ~ George Galloway

Logical Fallacies

The Logical Fallacy is a rhetorical device which has no grounding in actual fact and is used by people to unfairly gain the upper hand in debates. Being able to spot such a flaw goes a long way to invalidating an opponent's argument.

1. **Appeal to Complexity** – a form of **solipsism** whereby if the arguer doesn't understand the issue, then nobody does.

'It would be nice if it were that easy, but the truth is there's no easy answers to this question.'

'If think you're over-simplifying it. This is a actually a much more complex matter.'

2. **Appeal to False Authority** – referencing someone irrelevant in the hope that some credibility by association will rub off.

E.g. celebrities endorsing random products.

3. **Appeal to Fear** – bad things could happen. . . . small amounts of fear can be incredibly strong influences on people.

'If the boss heard you saying that, he would not be very happy.'

Preamble

Adapted from Wikipedia.

Violence is overt and intentional physically aggressive behaviour against another person. Warfare is large-scale organized violence carried out by one state against another. States also legitimately authorize the use of force through police power to maintain public order and uphold the rule of law. The causes of violent attitudes and behaviour are important topics of study in psychology and sociology. Obviously, violence has been practiced by humans since prehistoric times.

Stephen Pinker in his essay 'The History of Violence' offers evidence that on average, the amount and cruelty of violence to humans and animals has decreased over the last few centuries. He uses the example of the popular spectacle of cat burning in 16th century Paris – i.e. cruelty as entertainment. Human sacrifice, slavery, conquest and genocide, torture and the death penalty for misdemeanors, assassination, rape and murder were all common features of life for most of human history. Whereas today they are rare to non-existent in the West and far less common and much more widely condemned in the rest of the world.

The Facts:

1. Nevertheless, the WHO estimates that each year around 1.6 million lives are lost worldwide due to violence. It is among the leading causes of death for people ages 15-44, especially of males.
2. One in six youths in America between 10 and 17 has seen or knows someone who has been shot.
3. Violent crime in the US has increased by more than 600 percent since 1960.
4. The average child in the US watches 8,000 televised murders and 100,000 acts of violence before finishing elementary school. That number more than doubles by the time he / she reaches age 18.

Source: http://www.leaderu.com/orgs/probe/docs/violence.html

The topic of violence in popular media is controversial. This includes violence in:

- films
- television
- music
- comic books
- video games
- televised sports

Violence in the media has led to government censorship and regulation. In the United States the FCC regulates television and radio. Media also self-regulate, as through movie rating systems and the Entertainment Software Rating Board for video games. The question is however; is there really a strong link between the media and violence in society and would we still have a problem if there was total censorship of violent acts in the media?

Examples:

1. In April 1999, 18-year-old Eric Harris and 17-year-old Dylan Klebold killed 12 students and a teacher in the Columbine High School Massacre. The two were obsessed with the video game Doom, and before the shootings, Harris claimed that the massacre would be "like Doom".

2. In 2005, the American TV programme '60 Minutes' took on the case of 18-year old Devin Moore, wherein plaintiffs have argued 'Grand Theft Auto: Vice City' inspired him to kill three police officers that came to arrest him for stealing a car. At trial, the defense claimed that Moore had been inspired by the game although some have later pointed out that the defender would have said anything to avoid blame. A judge later sentenced the convicted killer to death by lethal injection.

3. In 2003, two American step brothers, Joshua and William Buckner, aged 14 and 16, respectively, used a rifle to fire at vehicles on Interstate 40 in Tennessee, killing a 45-year-old man and wounding a 19-year-old woman. The two shooters told investigators they had been inspired by *Grand Theft Auto III*.

4. In October 2004, a 41-year-old Chinese man named Qiu Chengwei stabbed 26-year-old Zhu Caoyuan to death over a dispute regarding the sale of a virtual weapon the two had jointly won in the game *Legend of Mir 3*.

5. In March 1972, a prosecutor at a trial of a 16-year-old boy accused of the manslaughter of one of his classmates referred to *A Clockwork Orange*, telling the judge that the case had a macabre relevance to the film.

    The attacker, a boy aged 16 from Bletchley, pleaded guilty after telling police that his friends had told him of the film "and the beating up of an old boy like this one"; defense counsel told the trial "the link between this crime and sensational literature, particularly *A Clockwork Orange*, is established beyond reasonable doubt."

6. In 1998 the infamous rap artist Tupac Shakur was murdered in a drive by shooting by gang headed by rival rap artist Notorious B.I.G – who himself was subsequently murdered in retaliation.

Debating Phrases

Concluding a point or argument

1. The simple truth is …
2. To draw a line under this debate, …
3. After careful consideration, we can conclude that ….
4. As you can see from our argument, …

Pollice Verso – Jean-Leon Gerome (1872)

This famous painting is not an entirely authentic depiction of a gladiator. In fact, this image invented the popular notion of the thumbs up, thumbs down gesture and the picture has played a big part in shaping modern conceptions of gladiatorial combat. It shows a group of vestal virgins in the crowd demonstrating particular blood lust in encouraging the fighter to execute his opponent.

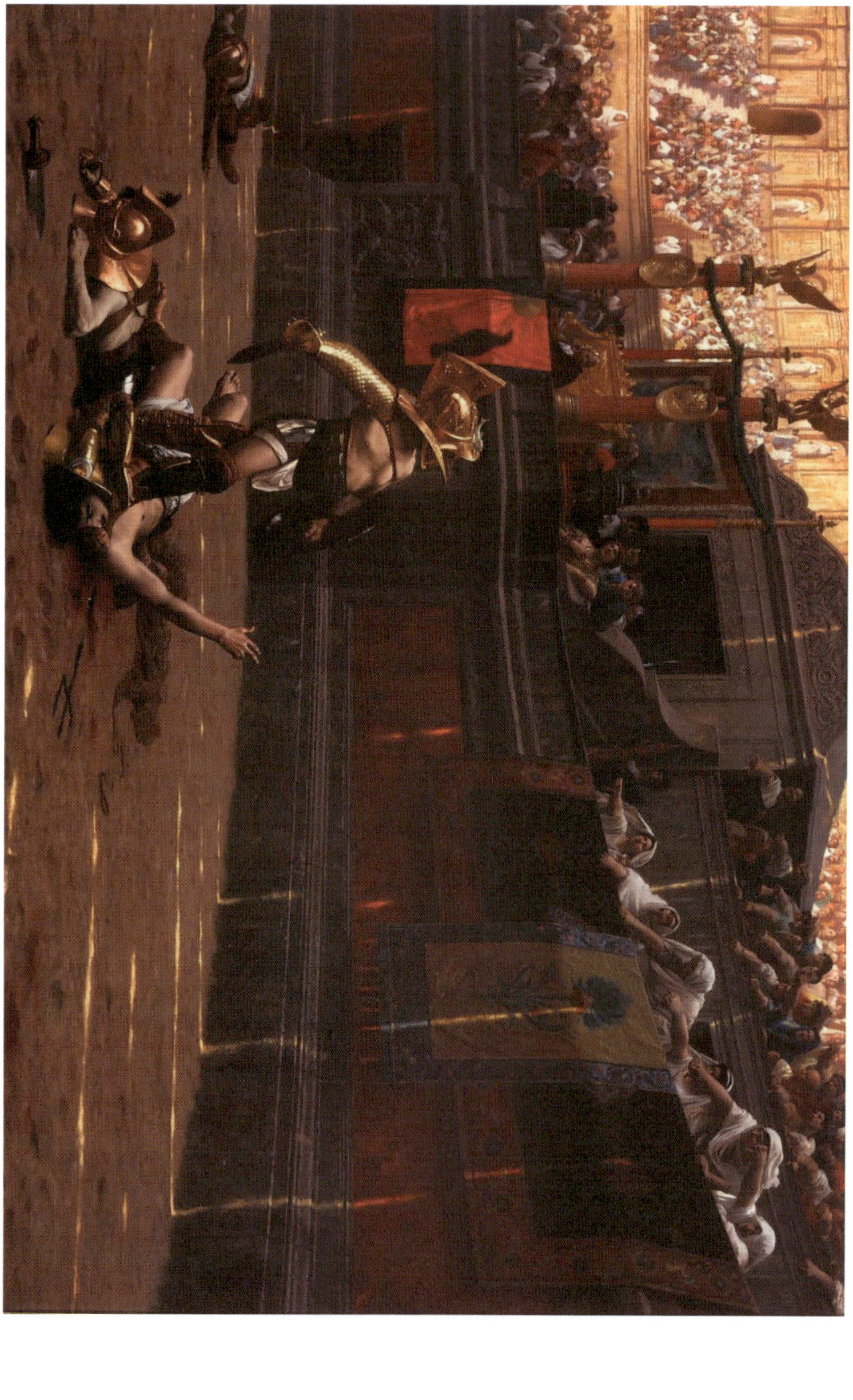

Great Debates

Society and the State are to Blame.

- Poverty is the root of it all. The government is not doing enough to stimulate the economy and create jobs. In the UK in the 1980s, violent crime and rioting were at very high levels because unemployment stood at 3 million. The government does not have proper laws to deal with violent crime and they are not doing enough to police the streets and stamp out gang activity.

- It's because of warlike and bullying leaders. Unjustified wars in places like Iraq mean people in society have fewer morals when it comes to conducting violence against each other. If it's ok for the government to lie about their reasons for violence internationally, then they are also making it acceptable at home among its citizens.

- Family values have degenerated in recent years with the increase in divorce driving kids to crime. If a strong male role model is not around the house, kids get into trouble. Prisons are full of people who have not had the benefit of a strong family upbringing. There is a 'Broken Society' / rotten culture where youths have little respect for anyone or anything because society is too liberal. We should return the old fashion way of dealing with hooligans – throw them in jail.

- The media alone is not enough to drive someone to murder. People who murder or cause violence must have a psychological instability to do such acts. People are born with these issues. The drive to aggression is largely biological / genetic and so this a matter of evolutionary psychology, not playing the 'blame game' with the media. The biological factor combines with circumstances outside of the person's control, to cause aggression. The media alone couldn't possibly drive people to go out and commit acts of violence. Therefore the media cannot take much of the blame for this. Society needs to care for people better psychiatrically.

- Music and media has always been blamed for being a dangerous influence on the youth going back to Elvis but it's really just human nature to commit acts of violence. Nothing to do with the media….

- People have attacked the media in the same way the tobacco industry was attacked in the 1990s; by greatly-exaggerating the effects of smoking on lung cancer. There is not enough direct causal evidence to link violence with the media. Most court cases trying to link violence with video games have failed in trying to prove this.

The Media are to Blame.

- Computer games glorify random killing and allow people to sharpen their killing skills, simulating the killing of hundreds or thousands of people in a single game. These games are basically **'murder simulators'** which harden children to unethical acts.

- If you look at the frequent shootings in US schools and universities, the murderers have spent endless hours playing shoot-em-up games and subsequently become desensitized to, and well-trained in, the act of killing. These shootings were just an extension of the game.

- Rap music glorifies murder and venerates murderers, making killing seem acceptable and even glamorous to young people. Tupac, the Notorious BIG and 50 Cent are to blame for making violence look cool. There is also a clear link between rap music and violence against women.

- TV and films are responsible because they model violent behaviour and people learn from this. People take inspiration from TV and films. TV increases arousal and aggressive thinking, beliefs and behaviours. TV has clearly maintained aggressiveness in society. To prove this you only have to get children to watch some violent show / film and then watch them playing aggressively and acting the scenes out with each other moments and even days later. I.e. wanting to be the hero / bad guy and wanting to carry a gun because it's 'cool' to fight enemies. This has been scientifically observed.

- Computer games like *Grand Theft Auto* are full of offensive content including drug use, graphic violence, sex, nudity, swearing and general criminal behaviour. Should we really be allowing children to access this? Video games have been scientifically proven to cause increases in bullying among the youth. Plus, video games these days are so realistic they worsen the problem.

- Books and movies are more to blame. A US Secret Service study found that only 12 percent of those involved in school shootings were attracted to violent video games, while 24 percent read violent books and 27 percent were attracted to violent films. Plus, an Australian study has found that only children with a natural feeling towards violence were affected by violent games.

Hostage Negotiation

A group of terrorist bombers have captured half of the students and are holding them hostage. The other half of the class represent police, government and general negotiators. There is a standoff situation. The bombers demand one million dollars in cash and a helicopter on the roof that will take them wherever they want. As well as this, they want food because they haven't eaten for more than 24 hours. The hostages have not eaten either. There is a growing mob of people gathering in the street outside, adding to the pressure-cooker atmosphere.

The government does not want to pay these villains anything, not just for monetary reasons but because it would show weakness and set a precedent, encouraging similar attempts. They will get some food if they release half of the hostages. They do not have a helicopter available and they do not have the authority to grant the bombers' security demands.

As well as getting the parties to communicate this situation to each other, ask each hostage to reason with their kidnappers as to why they should let him or her go instead of the others. In this way, one by one, each student has to plead his or her case and the kidnappers must decide which ones have the most worthy case.

Individual hostages should be given opportunities to speak to the negotiators (partly under duress) to tell them to give the terrorists what they want. Stockholm Syndrome could also come into play. In other words, the hostages begin speaking well of their captors and praise their motivations.

The negotiators have to think of what they can offer the bombers, while they must try to get as many concessions as they can. Each negotiator must take his or her turn to speak with the kidnappers. The mediators have to see what they can get the terrorists to do, and see if they can get them to release at least some of the hostages.

The main language focus is on using conditionals. The discussions must be creative, orderly and reasoned and the students must be given enough to time to prepare their arguments and demands, working as teams with leaders where necessary. Rifles should be improvised as props for the gang.

Various twists can be added to the scenario. For example, the bombers could be victims of some misfortune or injustice. They could be renegade cops, political dissidents or former colleagues of either party. Among other deals, there could be an exchange of people, family members and journalists can also be introduced. The bombers should also have varying levels of sympathy / ruthlessness, exposing cracks within the group which the negotiators must try to engineer and exploit.

Vocab Refresh

Battery – a crime involving the use of harmful contact and force against someone.

Assault – a crime causing a victim to fear violence against him / her.

The Media – conveys messages to large numbers of people, e.g. tv, books, newspapers, websites, etc.

Inspire – to plant the seed of belief or a new willingness to undertake great or meaningful things.

Slavery – a system where people are bought and sold and forced to work, often indefinitely.

Genocide – systematic mass murder on an ethnic or national basis.

Torture – the act of inflicting severe pain or a person or animal.

Assassination – the murder of a famous or important person.

Massacre – slaughter of a group of people or animals.

Hooliganism – general yobbery and brutishness, displayed frequently in relation to football fixtures.

Aggressive – hostile behaviour.

Offensive – something that causes disgust or displeasure.

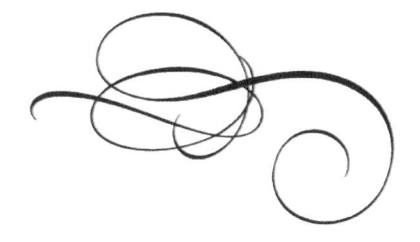

Debate 3 – Nature vs. Nurture

Debate 3 – Nature vs. Nurture

What is more important, nature or nurture?

Goals of the Lesson

- For students to become more familiar with the main points in the nature vs. nurture debate.
- For students to practice debating, using persuasive devices and functional phrases.
- For students to find some form of consensus on the issue.

Rhetoric

Discuss and demonstrate these figures of speech with the class and explain that people who are able to speak forcefully and persuasively often use devices like this. Tell the students that you would like them to try and use these devices during the debate.

1. **Anticlimax** – the arrangement of words in order of decreasing importance, often for comic effect.

'There are worse things in life than death. Have you ever spent an evening with an insurance salesman?' ~ Woody Allen.

2. **Anthimeria** – the substitution of one class of word for another, usually turning a noun into a verb, which is very easy to do in English.

Calvin: I like to verb words.
Hobbes: What?
Calvin: I take nouns and adjectives and use them as verbs. Remember when "access" was a thing? Now it's something you do. It got verbed. . . . Verbing weirds language.
Hobbes: Maybe we can eventually make language a complete impediment to understanding.
~ Bill Watterson, *Calvin and Hobbes*

3. **Anthropomorphism** – giving human characteristics to something. Similar to **zoomorphism**.

E.g. *Animal Farm* by George Orwell, *The Wind in the Willows* by Kenneth Grahame, *The Owl and the Pussycat* by Edward Lear.

Logical Fallacies

The Logical Fallacy is a rhetorical device which has no grounding in actual fact and is used by people to unfairly gain the upper hand in debates. Being able to spot such a flaw goes a long way to invalidating an opponent's argument.

1. **Appeal to Force** – some sort of threat; often a lawsuit or violence, or the prospect of burning in hell. Although a fallacy, the threat may be very much of a reality and has been an effective tactic of tyrants over the centuries.

'If you don't agree with us, you will go to prison.'

2. **Appeal to Widespread Belief** – *argumentum ad populum* – the bandwagon / peer pressure / common practice argument.

'Bribery is ok, everybody does it…'

3. **Argument by Fast Talking** – changing the subject so people don't have time to think about what was said.

Preamble

Adapted from Wikipedia.

The **Nature versus Nurture** debates concern the relative importance of an individual's innate qualities ('nature') versus personal experiences ('nurture') in determining or causing individual differences in physical and behavioral traits. The view that humans acquire all or almost all their behavioral traits from 'nurture' is known as *tabula rasa* ('blank slate').

This question was once considered to be an appropriate division of developmental influences, but since both types of factors are known to play such interacting roles in development, many modern psychologists consider the question naive – representing an outdated state of knowledge. Take this quote by the famous psychologist Donald Hebb.

Journalist Which, nature or nurture, contributes more to personality?
Hebb   Which contributes more to the area of a rectangle, its length or its width?

What are Traits?

Features of living things.
The heritable unit that may influence a trait is called a gene.

Definition

The definition of nurture has been expanded in order to include the influences on development arising from prenatal, parental, extended family and peer experiences, extending to influences such as media, marketing, and socio-economic status.

One way to determine the contribution of genes and environment to a trait is to study twins.

1. Identical twins reared apart are compared to randomly selected pairs of people. The twins share identical genes, but different family environments.
2. Identical twins reared together (who share family environment and genes) are compared to fraternal twins reared together (who also share family environment but only share half their genes).
3. Adoption study. Biological siblings reared together (who share the same family environment and half their genes) are compared to adoptive siblings (who share their family environment but none of their genes).

DR Lynn's Study

IQ and the Wealth of Nations is a controversial book written in 2002 by Dr Richard Lynn and Dr Tatu Vanhanen. Dr Lynn Claims that the East Asians (Chinese, Japanese and Koreans) have the highest mean IQ at 105. These are followed by the Europeans (IQ 100). Some way below these are the Inuit (Eskimos) (IQ 91), South East Asians (IQ 87), Native American Indians (IQ 87), Pacific Islanders (IQ 85), South Asians and North Africans (IQ 84). Well below these come the sub-Saharan Africans (IQ 67) followed by the Australian Aborigines (IQ 62). The least intelligent races are the Bushmen of the Kalahari Desert and the Pygmies of the Congo rain forests (IQ 54).

After ten chapters setting out evidence for each of the ten 'races' there follows a chapter on the reliability and validity of the measures. These show that the studies have high reliability in the sense that different studies of racial IQs give closely similar results. For instance, East Asians invariably obtain high IQs, not only in their own native homelands but in Singapore, Malaysia, Hawaii and North America. To establish the validity of the racial IQs he shows that they have high correlations with performance in the international studies of achievement in mathematics and science. Racial IQs also have high correlations with national economic development, providing a major contribution to the problem of why the peoples of some nations are rich and others poor. He argues further that the IQ differences between the races explain the differences in achievement in making the neolithic transition from hunter-gathering to settled agriculture, the building of early civilizations, and the development of mature civilizations during the last two thousand years. http://www.rlynn.co.uk/

Average IQ scores by country:

Hong Kong (PRC) 107	Germany 102	Belgium 100
South Korea 106	Italy 102	PRC 100
Japan 105	Netherlands 102	New Zealand 100
North Korea 105	Luxembourg 102	Singapore 100
Taiwan 104	Sweden 101	United Kingdom 100
Austria 102	Switzerland 101	

A Combination of Biology and Society

Consider this quote from psychologist Steven Pinker.

"Concrete behavioral traits that patently depend on content provided by the home or culture are not heritable at all: which language one speaks, which religion one practices, which political party one supports. But traits that reflect the underlying talents and temperaments are partially heritable: how proficient with language a person is, how religious, how liberal or conservative."

Obviously the real truth in this debate is that *both* 'nature' and 'nurture' contribute to a person's personality and behaviour. However leave this truism until the end of the debate (see 'Afterthought') because for the purpose of this class we want students to argue which is the biggest influence.

Debating Phrases

Addressing People

- Is the Speaker aware that...
- Mr / Madam Chairman...
- I request the floor...
- Are the Chair / the Speaker (not) aware that...
- Does the Speaker (not) agree that...?

Pygmalion And Galatea – Jean-Leon Gerome (1890)

Here is another painting by the artist featured in the previous lesson. The story of *Pygmalion* is an ancient Greek myth about an artist who rejects the advances of the women in the town where he lives. Instead, he spends all of his time in devoted to creating a statue of the most beautiful woman he can imagine. Finally, when the sculpture is completed, she comes to life and the two fall in love.

The story was famously adapted by George Bernard Shaw in the stage play of the same name and was then made into the musical *My Fair Lady*. In this version a poor London street girl called Eliza Doolittle is refined, mainly through accent reduction, into a lady of polite society. The story is a classic vindication of the socialist belief that all people are created equal and that environmental disadvantages can be eliminated through education.

Great Debates

'Nurture' is the most important factor in shaping personality.

- It is true that some cultures have qualities which are superior to other cultures. This has made more modern empires conquer primitive peoples and has led to the upward progress of mankind. These superior global cultures always originate from more northerly climates which by environmental necessity need to promote greater emphasis on teamwork, innovation and group security. This has nothing to do with genetics but everything to do with how a culture nurtures its society.

- IQ levels are often widely different among family members. Furthermore, IQ tests are not perfect; for example, they do not measure: wisdom, wit, creativity, interpersonal skills. A child who lacks nutrition will also have a lower IQ – this has nothing to do with inheritance and everything to do with environment. Furthermore, people who blame obesity on genetics are living in a dream world – there aren't many fat people in famine affected countries.

- Many successful people have been brought up in adverse circumstances. In fact, hardship is almost a prerequisite for success in life. Hardship is clearly an environmental influence and economic status shapes the behaviour and destiny of most of the world's population. Furthermore, you might be born with talents but if you don't use them they quickly drop away. Everybody in society is basically the same; some just have more opportunities than others.

- It is a ridiculous idea that a Jesus or a Hitler could be re-created through genetic cloning. Identical twins are genetically identical and, unlike the possible clones, share the same family environment, yet they are not identical in personality and other traits.

- Nurture is more important because the environment *causes* changes in the genetic make up of a society. If a population has lower IQs it is because they have not had the same access to nutrition throughout their history and so their brain size has not increased compared to that of richer societies. It seems natural that environmental conditions, over thousands of years, can cause genetic changes.

- Northern Europeans are taller the Asians and this is a genetic fact. However, the reason is because though history they developed a taste for red meat and dairy products much more so than Asians. Again this is a clear example of how environmental factors change genetics in a concrete way.

- Traditionally, people believed that human nature was not only inherited but decided by God. The differences between men and women were attributed to God's design. Whole ethnic groups were considered to be, by nature, superior or inferior. This was used to justify: slavery, racism, bigotry, imperialism. The Nazis believed that human nature was defined by race. The Communists, on the other hand, followed Marx's belief that human identity is a product of social structures, not nature.

'Nature' is the most important factor in shaping personality.

- It is proven beyond question that IQ is inherited – it is highly heritable. You are born with your basic intelligence, just as you are born with good looks or artistic ability. Of course it runs in the family, this is easily observable.

- People say that IQ is not a good measure of intelligence but IQ tests are the best measure of intelligence that we have. It is a fact that IQ results match with job performance, income and social status as well as health and longevity. The idea that 'All men are created equal' is a complete myth. Even a simple child knows that some men are fat, some thin, some tall, some small, some smart, some dumb.

- IQ also matches with brain size. Saying that a certain ethnic group has a higher IQ than another is just like saying the Dutch are the tallest people in the world. Nobody disputes this; it is just an interesting fact.

- In 1979 there was an experiment called the Minnesota study where 100 sets of twins were reared apart from each other. The study showed that 70 percent of the variance in IQ was associated with genetic variation. Studies have also shown that there are a number of genes that contribute to IQ differences. Furthermore, mutations of genes are associated with low IQ scores, especially the gene GD1 which is associated with an IQ of below 70. Claiming that mental traits have nothing to do with inheritance seems very unobservant and uninformed.

- It is well known that you cannot teach a person how to paint a good picture. Strange as it may sound, artistic ability is a gift (although this gift does need to be developed and practiced through childhood to come to true fruition). However, natural artistic flair is a highly heritable gift and you will usually find that if parents are artistically talented their offspring will exhibit this talent too.

- Psychologists should stress to parents the importance of supporting and building on a child's natural talents, rather than forcing them to participate in activities they don't enjoy or have a natural feeling towards.

- As we get older we become more like our parents. We are largely powerless to prevent this because usually we don't realize it. It takes other people to point this out. We develop the same tastes and opinions as our parents. Just as we look like them, we also behave in a similar way to our ancestors. We can see it clearly in our descendants.

- Doctors today will inform parents-to-be of any genetic conditions their unborn child may have. In a few decades, a genetic counselor will be able to tell parents whether an unborn child will have genetic leaning towards certain behaviours or characteristics.

- Maybe with the development of genetics in the future we can throw off the disgrace of scientific racism and instead be racial realists. Societies and governments can tailor social policy around accurate scientific knowledge of differences between races, if indeed they exist.

Afterthought

Being such a sensitive issue the teacher has to be careful of tempers flaring in this debate. But as teachers, we shouldn't shy away from controversial topics – students need to learn about the rights and wrongs of racial stereotyping and not just the folly but the misery of historical attempts to define people by race. The whole point of these classes is to get people to entertain ideas which are not their own and not to believe everything they hear. You should explain this to the students.

The real truth is that even though genetic differences do exist between individuals, on a racial scale these differences are non-existent. This was proven by the sequencing of the human genome. The differences we see exhibited by groups on a social scale boil down to the historical and cultural pressures we have lived under and the opportunities we have been given. An individual or a group is not inherently cleverer because of the colour of his or her skin.

The Forer Effect

Hand out the following text to each student and tell them you have written each one for them personally – i.e. the students think they are receiving unique descriptions. Ask them to read the statements using a dictionary. Then ask each student to rate from 1 to 5 how well the statement applies to themselves.

> You have a great need for other people to like and admire you. You can often be critical of yourself. You have a lot of potential which you have not used. While you have some personality weaknesses, you are usually able to compensate for them. Your sexual adjustment has presented problems for you. Disciplined and self-controlled outside, you tend to be worrisome and insecure inside. At times you have serious doubts about whether you have made the right decision or done the right thing. You prefer a certain amount of change and variety and become unhappy when restricted by limitations. You like to think of yourself as an independent thinker and do not accept others' statements without reasonable proof. You have found it unwise to be too frank in revealing yourself to others. At times you are extroverted, easy-going, sociable, while at other times you are introverted, cautious, reserved. Some of your hopes tend to be pretty unrealistic. Security is one of your major goals in life.

You should find that the students rate the text very highly in terms of it applying to themselves and this is indeed the principle behind horoscopes. The scientific term for this phenomenon is *subjective validation*. There is an inherent weakness (or cognitive bias) in people that causes us to easily believe what we wish to be true. Much the same might be said for people who harbour ideas on genetic superiority or determinism.

If you have time you may want to stretch out the exercise by asking students to write positive descriptions of the person next to them, just a few lines long, with as many adjectives as they can come up with. Then you can read them out while the class guesses the identities.

Vocab Refresh

Hereditary – the passing of something, often genetic traits, from parent to offspring.

Heritable – to have the potential to pass something from one generation to the next.

Trait – a characteristic or feature of something.

Inheritance – usually money or other wealth passed down to the next generation after death.

Genetic – adjective relating to genes and traits.

Inclination – propensity / likelihood of doing something or wanting to do something.

Influences – a force / power which affect and change behaviour.

Biological – relating to life and its processes.

Society – the system of humans living in some degree of mutual co-operation and relations, while sharing a culture or territory.

Partially – only somewhat. Not totally.

Temperament – a person or culture's natural disposition or personality and how much control they generally exercise over their emotions.

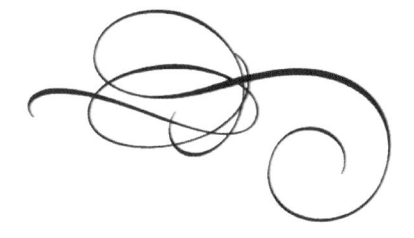

Debate 4 – Gun Control

Debate 4 – Gun Control

Gun Control: For or Against?

Goals of the Lesson

- For students to become more familiar with the concepts and arguments related to gun control.
- For students to practice debating, using persuasive devices and functional phrases.
- For students to find some form of consensus on the issue.

Rhetoric

Discuss and demonstrate these figures of speech with the class and explain that people who are able to speak forcefully and persuasively often use devices like this. Tell the students that you would like them to try and use these devices during the debate.

1. **Antimetabole** – repetition of words in successive clauses, in reverse order. Also known as **chiasmus**.

'Ask not what *your country* can do for *you*; ask what *you* can do for *your country*.' ~ John F. Kennedy

2. **Antiphrasis** – a word or words used contradictory to their usual meaning, often with irony.

'Here, under leave of Brutus and the rest –
For Brutus is an *honourable* man;
So are they all, all *honourable* men –
Come I to speak in Caesar's funeral.'
  ~ Shakespeare, *The Tragedy of Julius Caesar*

3. **Antithesis** – the juxtaposition of opposing or contrasting ideas.

'Brutus: Not that I loved Caesar less, but that I loved Rome more.' ~ Shakespeare, *The Tragedy of Julius Caesar*

Logical Fallacies

The Logical Fallacy is a rhetorical device which has no grounding in actual fact and is used by people to unfairly gain the upper hand in debates. Being able to spot such a flaw goes a long way to invalidating an opponent's argument.

1. **Argument by Generalization** – drawing a broad conclusion from a small number of perhaps unrepresentative cases.

'They say 1 out of every 5 people is Chinese. How is this possible? I know hundreds of people, and none of them is Chinese.' ~ Carl Sagan, *The Fine Art of Baloney Detection*

2. **Argument by Gibberish** – baffling people with complex or made up words, psychobabble or excessive jargon.

'Omniscience is greater than omnipotence, and the difference is two. Omnipotence plus two equals omniscience. META = 2.' ~ R. Buckminster Fuller, *No More Secondhand God*

'Each autonomous individual emerges holographically within egoless ontological consciousness as a non-dimensional geometric point within the transcendental thought-wave matrix.'

3. **Argument by Half Truth** – suppressing evidence to mislead the audience.

'I'm a really good driver. In the past thirty years, I have only had four speeding tickets.' This statement is true, but irrelevant if he or she started driving a week ago and has since accumulated four tickets.

Preamble

Adapted from Wikipedia.

The Second Amendment to the U.S. Constitution (1791) states

> 'A well regulated militia, being necessary to the security of a free state, the right of the people to keep and bear arms, shall not be infringed.'

Does this mean that everyone can carry a gun whenever they like or does it mean guns can only be used by a 'well regulated militia' for the purpose of keeping the freedom of the state?

Some statistics

- Approximately 9 or so children are killed by people discharging firearms every day across the US.

- Out of nearly 31,000 firearm-related deaths in the US 2005, suicides account for 55 percent whereas homicides account for 40 percent of deaths, accidents account for three percent, and the remaining two percent were legal killings.

- New Jersey adopted what sponsors described as 'the most stringent gun law' in the nation in 1966; two years later, the murder rate was up 46% and the reported robbery rate had nearly doubled.

- In 1976, Washington, D.C. enacted one of the most restrictive gun control laws in the nation. Since then, the city's murder rate has risen 134% while the national murder rate has dropped 2%.

- Among the 15 states with the highest homicide rates, 10 have restrictive or very restrictive gun laws.

- Twenty percent of U.S. homicides occur in four cities with just 6% of the population – New York, Chicago, Detroit and Washington, D.C. – and each has a virtual prohibition on private handguns.

- UK banned private ownership of most handguns in 1997, previously held by an estimated 57,000 people – 0.1% of the population. Since 1998, the number of people injured by firearms in England and Wales has more than doubled.

- The number of firearms available in the US was 223 million in 1995.

- About 25% of the adults in the United States personally own a gun, the vast majority of them men.

- And, about half of the adult U.S. population lives in households with guns.

- Less than half of gun owners say that the primary reason they own a gun is for self-protection against crime, reflecting a popularity of hunting and sport-shooting among gun owners.

- As hunting and sport-shooting tends to favor rural areas, naturally the bulk of gun owners generally live in rural areas and small towns.

Debating Vocab

Introduce these relevant words and stress that you would like students to speak as formally as possible while debating.

- the house — all the delegates
- the floor — when talking about the floor, we actually mean the right to speak
- to yield the floor — to give the right to speak to somebody.
- out of order — forbidden

The Duel Between Alexander Hamilton and Aaron Burr (1804)

Duelling with pistols, rather than swords, had become something of a craze in eighteenth century England. This custom persisted for some time in the early United States, long after becoming an illegal and taboo practice across the Atlantic. Many men of social status felt it proper to resolve disputes through duels. Such disputes were often of an extraordinarily petty nature by today's standards. Duelling was considered a fitting and courageous way of safeguarding one's honour.

Founding Father and first Treasury Secretary, Alexander Hamilton was killed from a pistol shot fired by his long-term adversary Aaron Burr, following a perceived insult and exchange of heated letters. The location in New Jersey where the duel took place was the same spot in which Hamilton's son had been killed three years earlier. The duel took place at dawn and Hamilton fired the first shot but missed, apparently on purpose. Burr showed no mercy and promptly fired a bullet straight into his midriff. This callous response violated the accepted etiquette of duelling at the time, where death was to be avoided if at all possible.

The engraving opposite, though a famous depiction, seems somewhat anachronistic given the size of the weapons the men are holding compared to the extended barrels of typical flintlock pistols of the day, and indeed the ones the men actually used.

Great Debates

No, gun ownership should not be controlled.

- Self defence – individual and collective. The right to bear arms originates in both US and UK law with the 1689 Bill of Rights. Oppressive governments like Nazis, USSR and Apartheid South Africa all introduced bans on gun ownership. Self defence is a fundamental and basic human right closely related to the right to life. Gun control is therefore unethical.

- Gun control only disarms the people who will <u>not</u> commit crimes. Criminals will always find a way to get guns or weapons. Gun control is bad for victims and better for criminals. It encourages rather than prevents murders because it is easy to attack an unarmed man. People who defend themselves with guns will not be injured or lose property. People without guns who resist or do not resist will be hurt.

- Guns allow the population to limit the power of government, to prevent dictators taking control. Therefore guns equal freedom and equality. Take this quote by Abraham Lincoln: "This country, with its institutions, belongs to the people who inhabit it. Whenever they shall grow weary of the existing Government, they can exercise their constitutional right of amending it or their revolutionary right to dismember or overthrow it."

- People who talk about the thousands of children killed every year forget that they are usually late-teenagers in gangs involved in drugs and crime – hardly innocent children. Guns don't kill people, people kill people. A gun in itself is a neutral object. Cars kill more people than guns, but we don't ban cars.

- The safety paradox. Guns make people feel safer. If guns were banned, people would go back to using swords and if swords were banned people would immediately start using rocks. Violence in inherent in human nature therefore being armed means being at peace.

- During the Middle Ages, there was a high level of weapon ownership among the Japanese population. This stopped the Japanese Imperial government establishing totalitarian control. The beauty of America is that no one and no state can take your property away from you. This is the reason why America is the freest country in the world.

- Banning guns will create a black market. There are already too many guns in circulation to make a ban possible. Plus in the UK where there is a problem with illegal guns, gun crime has actually risen since the handgun ban in 1997.

Yes, gun ownership should be controlled.

- Automatic guns make the argument for hand gun use outdated. In the 18th century, guns (flintlock pistols) were unreliable, inaccurate and took a long time to 'prepare'. The right to bear arms originates with duelling which was a semi-legal way to settle disputes of honour in antiquated society.

- The Constitution was written 300 years ago. Now, automatic handguns mean that many people can be easily killed over the smallest disputes. An angry wife could just suddenly snap one day and turn on her husband with an automatic handgun. He would have no chance of survival and therefore automatic handguns are morally wrong and have no fair reason to exit in a modern society.

- Regulation can stop guns getting into the wrong hands. If guns are lying around the house there is more chance they will get used, especially by children. Suicides are also more likely to happen. People who say cars kill more than guns are forgetting that cars have another purpose whereas guns do not.

- During a year when over 5,000 teens and children died from gun wounds in the USA, in Great Britain, where gun ownership is very restricted, 19 teens and children died from gun wounds.

- The availability of guns encourages random killing – e.g. the high school shootings in the US. America has an unhealthy gun culture. Guns are shown frequently in movies, television, music, books, and magazines. The origins of this go back to the early settlers who really needed guns, but in modern society they should be banned.

- If people need protect themselves and their country, what better then a rifle? Hand guns make no sense in an invasion / military situation. Switzerland requires every male over the age of 20 to keep a rifle and 20 rounds of ammunition in their home. Switzerland is one of the safest countries in the world.

- Statistics show than guns are responsible for about 10,000 murders in the US every year, China by comparison has a much larger population but far fewer murders. The problem is that the gun lobby in America are too politically powerful but they do not serve the interests of the wider population.

Assassinations

Mention that four of America's presidents have been assassinated and many more attempts have been made on others. Then discuss the murder of Kennedy by a sniper bullet in 1963 on a visit to Dallas. See how much the students can tell you about it. Put the key facts and ideas on the board. You might also mention that Bobby Kennedy was assassinated five years later but as with the JFK shooting, mystery still surrounds the case and conspiracies abound.

Lee Harvey Oswald was arrested in suspicion of the killing but by a peculiar and frustrating twist on his arrest, a local businessman Jack Ruby suddenly appeared and fired a shot into his stomach, killing him.

Ask each student each to write 5 questions they would ask Oswald if they had the opportunity to question him about the assassination. Then once this is completed ask students to swap their papers with their partner and role play the interviews at the front of the class.

Vocab Refresh

Homicide – another (latinate) name for murder.

The right to bear arms – the second amendment to the US constitution.

Totalitarian – a system whereby the government exercises full control over nearly every aspect of its citizens' lives

Constitution – the fundamental laws of a country that establish it as a state. This word has other meanings including the physical character and strength of a person's body or simply what something is made up from.

Paradox – something which is true, when its inversion would seem more likely. E.g. possessing weapons actually creates peace.

Firearm – a ballistic weapon (guns and also grenade launchers) than can be carried about your person. Typically a pistol.

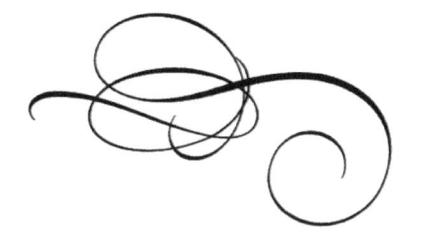

Debate 5 – Distribution of Wealth

Debate 5 – Distribution of Wealth

The growing gap between rich and poor – what's to be done?

Goals of the Lesson

- For students to become more familiar with the causes of and solutions to income inequality.
- For students to practice debating, using persuasive devices and functional phrases.
- For students to find some form of consensus on the issue.

Rhetoric

Discuss and demonstrate these figures of speech with the class and explain that people who are able to speak forcefully and persuasively often use devices like this. Tell the students that you would like them to try and use these devices during the debate.

1. **Antonomasia** – the substitution of a phrase for a proper name or vice versa. As Charlotte Higgins said in her analysis of Barack Obama's use of rhetoric, "Antonomasia sets up an intimacy between speaker and audience, the flattering idea that we all know what we are talking about without need for further exposition."

'The King' aka Elvis Presley.

'A young preacher from Georgia' ~ Barack Obama referring to Martin Luther King.

2. **Aphorism** – a tersely phrased statement of a truth or opinion, an adage.

'That which does not destroy us makes us stronger.' ~ Friedrich Nietzsche

3. **Aphorismus** – statement that calls into question the definition of a word.

'How can you call yourself a man?'

Logical Fallacies

The Logical Fallacy is a rhetorical device which has no grounding in actual fact and is used by people to unfairly gain the upper hand in debates. Being able to spot such a flaw goes a long way to invalidating an opponent's argument.

1. **Argument by Laziness** – uninformed opinion.

2. **Argument by Pigheadedness** – refusing to admit something despite incontrovertible evidence to the contrary.

Bill   Look, it's raining outside.
Dave   Don't be ridiculous, of course it's not.

3. **Argument by Prestigious Jargon** – e.g. psychobabble – using big complicated words so that you will seem to be an expert.

'The differences between these modes of intervention is that in the case of linguistics applied the assumption is that the problem can be reformulated by the direct and unilateral application of concepts and terms deriving from linguistic enquiry itself. That is to say, language problems are amenable to linguistics solutions. In the case of applied linguistics, intervention is crucially a matter of mediation . . . applied linguistics . . . has to relate and reconcile different representations of reality, including that of linguistics without excluding others.' ~ Henry Widdowson, *On The Limitations of Linguistics Applied*

Preamble

The GINI Index is used to measure income disparity / equality.

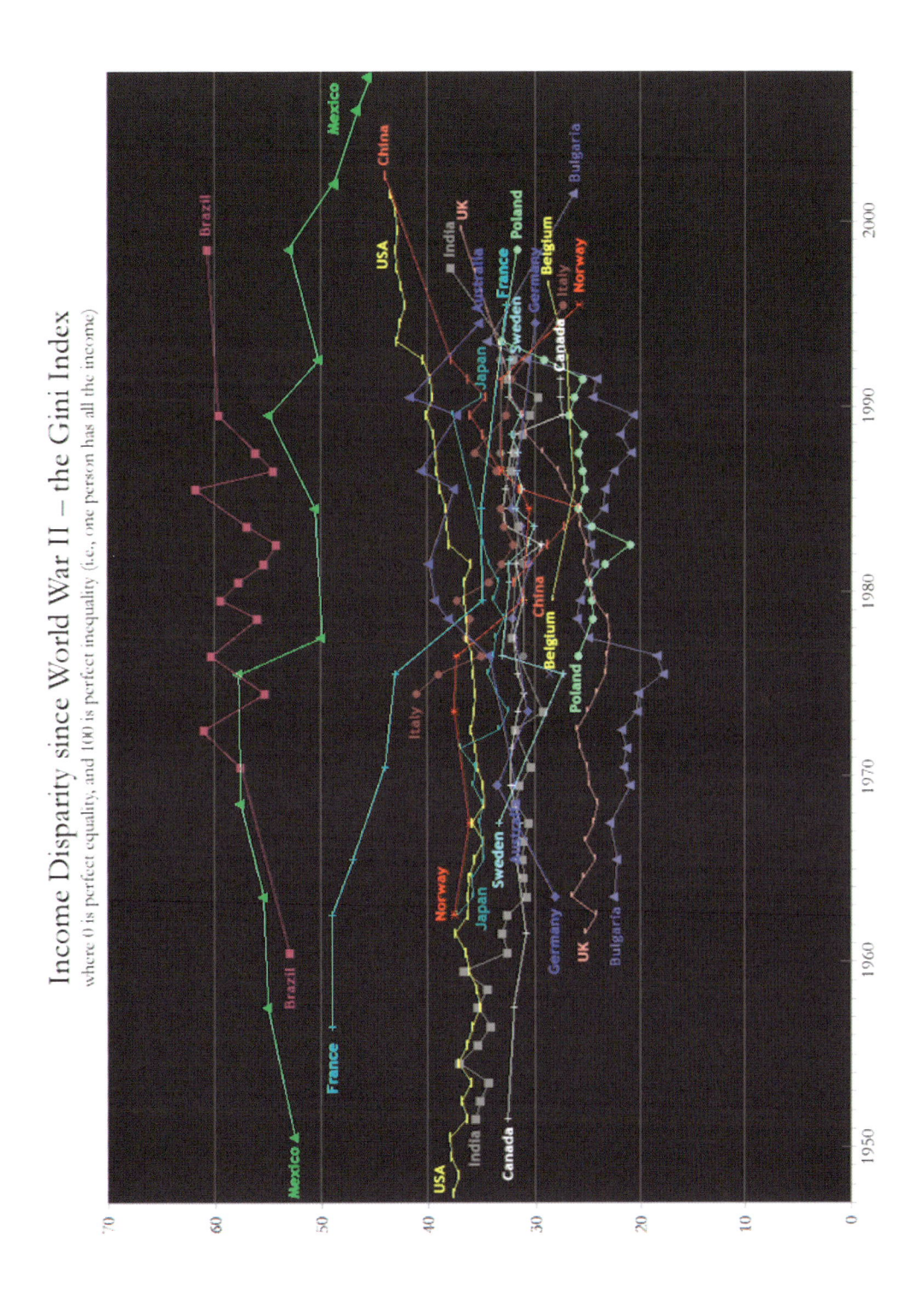

Income Disparity since World War II – the Gini Index
where 0 is perfect equality, and 100 is perfect inequality (i.e., one person has all the income)

If you look at the graph, Brazil is miles above every other country in income inequality. This is because Brazil's land and wealth is mostly held in the hands of a few privileged families. Brazil is also largely an export nation which gains its income from the sale of raw materials and foodstuffs. Thus Brazil is traditionally a high inflation, cash economy.

The Western European Nations by contrast (Germany, Sweden, Italy, Norway, as well as Canada) have traditionally been strong socialist societies with high taxation and relative income equality. The economies of these countries are characterized by being highly industrialized with strong prevalence of small and medium-sized high-tech manufacturing and service businesses constituting the solid base of the economy.

The Anglo-Saxon economies; United States, Britain, Australia where taxation and state protection are generally lower, and home ownership higher, are further up the inequality scale. America has always had fairly high income inequality.

China having started off in 1980 from a very middling position is now on a par with the United States in terms of stark income inequality. Note in the United States' and UK inequality has steadily risen since the free-market policies of Regan / Thatcher in the 80s which were business-friendly, tax cutting, low welfare (Reaganomics). Canada and Japan by contrast has hardly moved off the center ground for the last 50 years.

China

China contains one fifth of the world's population and is in the ascendancy to become the world's leading economic superpower. This will give the country an enormous responsibility and influence in the world. However, economists have reported that the growing gap between rich and poor is reaching dangerous levels which could lead to social unrest. Since the 'reform and opening up' under Deng Xiaoping, China has gone from an 'iron rice bowl' economy where people were guaranteed jobs for life to pursuing a policy of 'socialism with Chinese characteristics'. In other words; Capitalism.

The Party seems to have wholeheartedly adopted the philosophy that 'if you are not a communist after 30 years, you don't have a heart but if you are not a capitalist after 30 years, you don't have a brain.'

The propagation of a 'Me' society has made China prosper and migrant workers have flooded into the cities. By giving hard working and talented people the freedom to get rich there is now a nouveau riche living in luxury villas squeezed between migrants searching in trash cans for plastic bottles and living in shacks. At the same time however, China is unique in having pulled more people out of poverty in such a short time, than any country in history. Still, more than 30 million Chinese live in absolute poverty.

Nowadays the affluent one-fifth of China's population earn 50 percent of total income, with the bottom one-fifth taking home 4.7 percent. This trend looks like widening further. It is a far cry from when Mao Zedong and the Communist Party seized land from wealthy farmers and nationalized private businesses in one of the greatest leveling campaigns ever undertaken.

Could income inequality be the next flashpoint?

Debating Vocab

Decorum	Latin for 'silence', 'be quiet'
Motion	formal proposal
To raise a point	to say something of value in the argument
To rise	to stand up (e.g. "Sri Lanka, please rise and state your point.")

Chinese Cultural Revolution Propaganda

The Chinese Cultural Revolution was a period lasting from the late 1960s to the late 70s when, under the twilight years of Mao Zedong's leadership, the country began on a course a regression and persecution of middle class intellectuals. Until recent years, Chinese society was broadly and evenly impoverished. This meant that people demonstrated a stronger sense of community and togetherness than the more individualistic and competitive society that now characterizes much of the country. The propaganda from this period is highly distinctive yet copied from the typical Soviet idealistic illustrations which, incidentally, were also the main inspiration for the iconic British children's book publisher, Ladybird.

In this poster entitled 'A Celebration from Industry', Chinese workers of all descriptions are portrayed as being in harmonious unison and working selflessly and industriously towards the building of a better China. The soldier in the background is the iconic and almost mythical Lei Feng, who was and still is promoted by the Communist Party as being the archetypal good citizen – not unlike a Jesus figure, with incorruptible character demonstrating immaculate behaviour towards others and undying commitment to the revolution.

Great Debates

I'm in favour of laissez-faire.

- The 'trickle-down' is best. Without rich people, poor people wouldn't have jobs. A welfare society removes individuals' initiative and discourages business owners from creating new jobs because of all the benefits they have to pay. I believe in Capitalism – in capitalism as in life, there are winners and losers. There should be no minimum wage because it makes our country less competitive globally.

- It's more natural to just leave resources to allocate themselves. The market might have winners and losers in the short term but in the long term society as a whole can prosper with as few restrictions on trade as possible – just like Hong Kong. 'Sink or swim' makes a stronger society, just like Darwinism. Greed is good – it has marked the upward surge of mankind. I believe in competition and the profit motive! Let market forces do their work.

- Some people don't want to work – they are lazy, so why should the taxpayer help them out by paying welfare benefits? Why should the government give them handouts? They should get nothing – to make them realize that there are no free lunches in this world. Pennies don't come from heaven; they have to be earned here on earth!

- The individual is key – leave the decision making power with him or her. People know how to make money better than the state does. The market is efficient and the government shouldn't interfere with it. If we let the rich get richer, everyone benefits. If the government supports the population too much, they will become weak and dependent.

- Even if individual businessmen make many mistakes in their investment decisions, the overall economy can still be healthy. But if the government makes some small mistakes in their planning there can be all sorts of trouble for the whole economy, e.g. shortages of basic goods and public services. This means wasted taxpayers' money.

- The problem with taxes is that the rich don't pay them. They hide their money which is even worse for the economy. So by reducing taxes the rich will put that money back into the economy. Therefore more goods are produced and prices get cheaper. The poor always benefit from increases in GDP. This is called the horse and sparrow theory. If you feed the horse enough oats, some will pass through to the road for the sparrows.

I'm in favour of government action.

- Welfare reforms have been necessary in all industrialized nations because the market has failures. Economies go into recessions and slumps and only the government has the power to fix that. The opposition are arguing for a 'do nothing' approach to solve the gap between rich and poor. This is an absurd, selfish and irresponsible suggestion.

- Sweden is the model of a welfare sate and successful socialist society. The economy is high tech and the labour force is highly skilled. The country boasts excellent communications and generous welfare spending achieved through high tax rates. This is true of all the Scandinavian countries.

- Sweden's system of welfare benefits means they have the one of the highest standards of living in the world. If it works for them, why can't it work for us? Higher taxation and spending programs are the answer.

- It's morally right to look after the weaker members of society, especially if they cannot look after themselves. Workers need to school their children. Workers need rights so their bosses don't run away without paying them. Old people need heating in winter and protection from crime. Unemployed people need skills training and benefits to find work. Handicapped people need care. Nurses and coal miners are the most important people in society but their incomes need to be subsidized. Children need medical care and investment in schools. Poor people need self-esteem.

- The UK under Thatcher created a 'me' society where the weakest got screwed. We are going the same way. This country used to be an 'us' society where (even though nobody had much) people were closer, communities were stronger and old folk were looked after. Now that's all changing – people are more selfish these days and it's ethically wrong.

- Failing to do something about the growing gap between rich and poor could lead to civil unrest because the economy is volatile and people are not happy or secure. There could be riots in the streets if we ignore their plight.

- The group is key, not the individual. A rising tide floats all boats. Growth comes from the bottom up, not the top down – the demand side, not the supply side. Society should level the playing field to create fairness and more opportunity for disadvantaged people.

- China is a good example. There are too many people in China and not enough jobs, so wages are low. Meanwhile, Chinese labour law is not respected by many factory owners. Migrant workers are mistreated. Rich people should be taxed more and the middle class less.

- Greed is wrong and the disparity in this country is already shocking. In any modern society the following measures should be provided by a responsible government: minimum wage, laws to force companies to provide welfare for their employees, welfare programs like state pensions, unemployment and housing benefit, anti-monopoly laws, subsidies for businesses and farmers, infrastructure.

The Root of Some Good

Ask the students to list ten things they would do if they won a million dollars. Compare answers and reasons as a class.

Then put students into groups and tell them that they now have a million dollars to spend, but you want to know three things:

- How much will go to charity?
- Which single cause will they give to?
- Why do they choose this cause above so many others?

The groups must come to consensus. After the discussions, list the causes on the board. Now ask each group to think of five ways in which they could raise money for these causes.

Make it real. Put the best or most practical activities into action and see how much money each group can make.

Vocab Refresh

Nouveau riche – a person who is newly rich and overtly ostentatious.

Laissez-faire – meaning 'leave it be' – a policy (usually economic) of freedom and non-interference (in markets and in the ability of people to do business). Popularized by the teachings of Adam Smith.

Welfare – financial or other assistance to an individual or family from a city, state, or national government.

Subsidy – a government payment made to assist a company.

Disparity – inequality, unevenness.

Unrest – civil violence / rioting.

Infrastructure – roads, bridges, tunnels, phone cables, etc.

Disharmony – social equality.

The Welfare State – a country with high taxation and strong government intervention & assistance.

The trickle-down effect – the idea that encouraging rich people to spend and invest via tax breaks, creates money, goods and jobs for the poor. Like water trickling down a mountain, it all reaches the bottom eventually. Many claim that this idea is usually a fallacy when applied to a country's fiscal policy.

Migrant worker – in the Chinese context, a person who moves from the inland or rural provinces, with few resources and the intention of finding work and bettering their situation in the city – usually one of the coastal cities.

Level playing field – a fair situation where everyone has the same rules and the same chances to win.

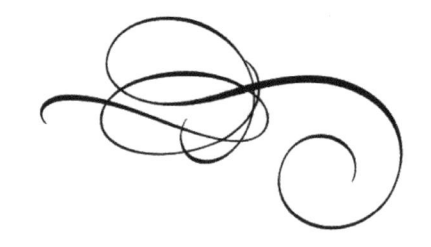

Debate 6 – Healthcare

Debate 6 – Healthcare

Universal Healthcare: For or Against?

Goals of the Lesson

- For students to become more familiar with the arguments for and against state healthcare.
- For students to practice debating, using persuasive devices and functional phrases.
- For students to find some form of consensus on the issue.

Rhetoric

Discuss and demonstrate these figures of speech with the class and explain that people who are able to speak forcefully and persuasively often use devices like this. Tell the students that you would like them to try and use these devices during the debate.

1. **Apophasis** – mentioning an idea by not mentioning it. A disingenuous denial, an overt insinuation or a cutting backhanded compliment. Also called **paralepsis** and closely related to **epanorthosis**.

'I pass over the fact that Jenkins beats his wife, is an alcoholic, and sells dope to kids, because we will not allow personal matters to enter into our political discussion.'

2. **Aporia** – deliberating with oneself, often with the use of **rhetorical questions**.

E.g. Hamlet's soliloquy.

3. **Aposiopesis** – breaking off or pausing speech for dramatic or emotional effect.

'Get out, or else…!'

Logical Fallacies

The Logical Fallacy is a rhetorical device which has no grounding in actual fact and is used by people to unfairly gain the upper hand in debates. Being able to spot such a flaw goes a long way to invalidating an opponent's argument.

1. **Argument by Question** – asking long-winded or loaded questions.

'Have you stopped beating your wife?'

'How can scientists expect us to believe that anything as complex as a single living cell could have arisen as a result of random natural processes?' ~ Don Lindsay, *A List of Fallacious Arguments*

2. **Argument by Repetition** – *argumentum ad nauseam* – if you say something often enough, some people will begin to believe it.

Any form of brainwashing. Speeches by Hitler are good examples.

3. **Argument by Rhetorical Question** – asking a question which deliberately leads to you desired answer.

Why should merely cracking down on terrorism help to stop it, when that method hasn't worked in any other country? Why are we so hated in the Muslim world? What did our government do there to bring this horror home to all those innocent Americans? And why don't we learn anything, from our free press, about the gross ineptitude of our state agencies? about what's really happening in Afghanistan? about the pertinence of Central Asia's huge reserves of oil and natural gas? about the links between the Bush and the bin Laden families? ~ Mark Crispin Miller, *Brain Drain*

Preamble

Adapted from Wikipedia.

'Care for the British people from cradle to grave' was the slogan of the founders of the world's first publicly funded healthcare system in 1948. The NHS has been described as one of the greatest social achievements of the 20th century. In all wealthy industrialized countries today, public funding covers the cost of medical, dental and mental healthcare – the big exception for the moment being the United States. There is also a worldwide trend in developing countries to provide this service.

A universal system should include GPs (qualified doctors), health centers and clinics, hospitals, ambulance services, advice services, dentistry, and free prescriptions. Countries implement such programs through legislation and taxation. The UK operates a system where care is free at the point of need. However, critics point to

- overblown bureaucracy
- unresponsive services
- too much political control

Nevertheless, British people live longer and healthier, and are financially better off than they were sixty years ago. Current NHS expenditure is around £90 billion per year.

China is undertaking a reform on its health care system, particularly to make it more affordable for the rural poor. The annual cost of medical cover is 50 yuan per person. Of that, 20 yuan is paid in by the central government, 20 yuan by the provincial government and a contribution of 10 yuan is made by the patient. As of September 2007, around 80 percent of the whole rural population of China had signed up (about 685 million people).

Most developed countries also have a small private healthcare system but private firms do not usually provide AIDS / HIV care, birth control, and services for conception / sexual problems and sex change, learning difficulties, behavioural and developmental problems, pregnancy and childbirth.

In 2007 the American political activist Michael Moore, filmed a documentary entitled Sicko in which he investigated the dilapidated state of the US healthcare system and compared it with that of Canada, the UK, France and Cuba.

According to Sicko, almost fifty million Americans are uninsured and 18,000 people will die each year because of no insurance, while those who are covered are often victims of insurance company fraud and red tape. In addition, America ranks last in the infant mortality list of the 23 industrialized nations.

Moore basically portrays opponents of universal healthcare as products of 1950s-style anti-communist propaganda. He then shows that socialized public services like police, fire service, postal service, public education and community libraries have not led to communism in America. In the UK, Moore then discovers that not only is healthcare completely free, but pharmaceuticals are free for the young and old and heavily discounted for everyone else, while hospitals operate a cashier desk to reimburse people for travel costs and other out-of-pocket expenses incurred by low-income patients. He then interviews British MP Tony Benn who claims that dismantling the NHS would be the equivalent of repealing women's suffrage and would result in a revolution.

Returning to the United States, interviews disclose that 9/11 rescue workers who volunteered after the September 11, 2001 attacks were denied government funds to care for physical and psychological maladies they subsequently developed, including respiratory disease and Post Traumatic Stress Disorder. Unable to receive and afford medical care in the U.S., the 9/11 rescue workers, as well as all of Moore's friends in the film needing medical attention, sail from Miami to Cuba on three speedboats in order to obtain free medical care provided for the enemy combatants detained at Guantanamo Bay.

Later US Developments

In 2010 President Obama managed to institute a reform and subsidization of the somewhat corrupted system of healthcare insurance in the United States, making it easier, and in fact mandatory, for poor and unwell people to receive insurance and taxing the providers to eliminate waste and profiteering.

The health care bill does not permit federal funding for abortion and the option for allowing insurance cover for abortions at all is a matter for individual states to decide.

Debating Phrases

<u>Arguing</u>

This is *not* about ...., this *is* about ....
We need to make sure that ....
Not only is .... but ....
Isn't it clear that ....
Isn't it true that ....

Hôtel Dieu in Paris (1500)

The Hotel Dieu is the oldest hospital in Paris. It was founded in 651 and continues to be a functioning hospital today. For most of its history the hospital relied entirely on charity and the Church, being run by nuns and funded by wealthy patrons who felt obliged to atone for their sins by giving to the needy. You can see in the picture that the sick are separated from the relatively well and nuns in the forefront are sewing up the body bags of the recently deceased; possibly plague victims.

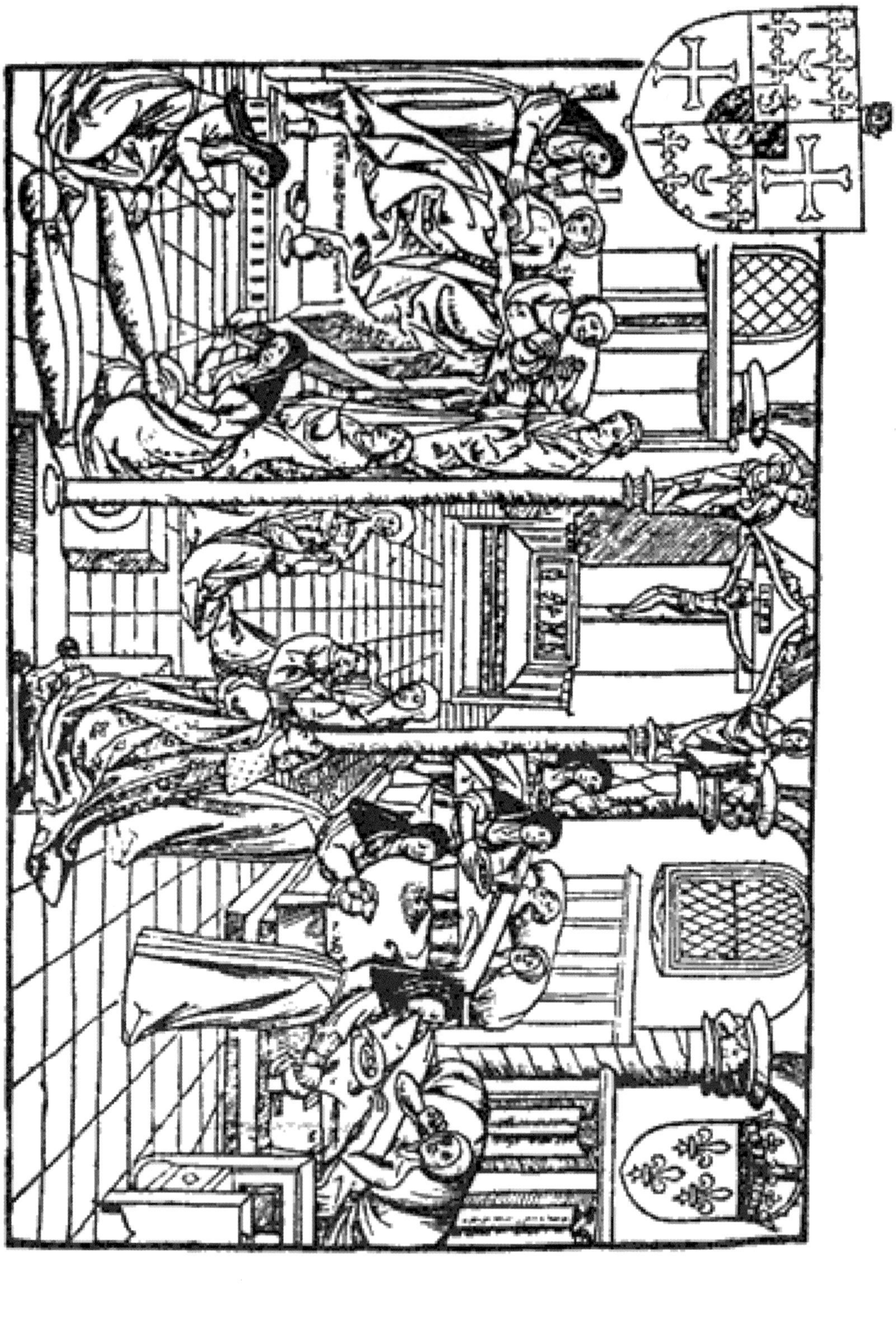

Yes. I'm in favour of universal healthcare.

- A healthy country is a wealthy country. People would be more productive and more willing to take business risks. The economy also needs a safety net for the weaker members of society; the young, the old, the undereducated and the unemployed. It would create a society of more equal opportunity. Healthcare costs are unpredictable because you never know when you will get sick. If we remove this chance of unfairness and misfortune from society, we will protect and strengthen our people.

- A majority of taxpayers and citizens would prefer a universal healthcare system. How is it any different from education? If we don't do this then we are putting ourselves at a disadvantage because all the other countries are doing it. They will have stronger, healthier, wealthier populations than we do. In America, 45 percent of all bankruptcies are related to medical bills. In globally competitive world, universal healthcare is more important than ever.

- The profit motive affects the cost and quality of health care. If hospitals are a business they will want to make the most money for the least work. They will not care for people as well as they should and the free market means that those who can't afford care, won't get it. Right now China and America have higher infant mortality and lower life expectancy than many other countries. This is unacceptable.

- Healthcare is a basic human need because you cannot live without it. Then is it not a basic human right? How can we call ourselves a modern country if we don't have universal healthcare? By providing this benefit the government is taking a moral stance. It also shows the world that we have a superior culture and a better political system, because we really care for our fellow citizens.

- Should we just let the handicapped struggle with no assistance? Not everyone is unhealthy because of their lifestyle. Some people have genetic reasons why they are ill. Should we exclude these people from society? NO, that's what Hitler would do. The fact is that no-one has 100 percent control over their health. You can't blame people for having bad health.

- Even if taxes went up, we would not have to pay any insurance premiums and wages would increase because employers would not need to pay premiums. People would not abuse the system by taking more care than they need because people do not consume healthcare like candy. On the other hand, people would seek preventative care much earlier if it was free.

- Universal health care could help businesses because they have to pay insurance for their workers. The Big Three U.S. car manufacturers said health-care was a reason for their financial troubles. The cost of health insurance to U.S. car manufacturers adds between $900 and $1,400 to each car.

No. I'm not in favour of universal healthcare.

- Healthcare is not a right. It is not the responsibility of government to provide healthcare. If the state provided healthcare as a benefit, it would eventually be taken as a 'right' by the public and then it would be impossible to control or remove.

- People should just take care of themselves. Why should it be the government or the taxpayer's responsibility to provide healthcare for people who can't live a healthy lifestyle? If someone is not insured, it's their fault. Period. Why should I care about them?

- Universal healthcare would mean long waiting lists, shortages and poor quality of care, which could result in unnecessary deaths. Also, people would consume more drugs that they don't really need but they take because it's free. Healthy people who take care of themselves will have to pay for the burden of those who smoke, are obese, etc. Why should I pay someone's drug addiction? Lazy people just abuse the system a get a free ride. We all know it, but everyone is too polite to say so.

- Universal healthcare would reduce efficiency because there would be more bureaucracy and paperwork. There isn't a single government department that runs efficiently so do we really want the state running something as big as healthcare for the whole population?

- Profit motives, competition, and individual risk have always led to greater cost control and effectiveness. The free market is the best solution. Universal healthcare would basically be one big government handout. What a waste of money. There is nothing wrong with the system we have right now. Furthermore, if private healthcare companies don't make profits to invest in R&D, innovation in medicine will slow.

- Many countries have aging populations, which means much more will have to be spent on healthcare. Some countries also face booming populations, making the project unworkable. Free healthcare is not really free; it puts stress on the system and the taxpayer. Without increasing taxes, expenses would have to come from cuts in other areas such as defence or education.

- PriceWaterhouseCoopers say that global healthcare spending will triple in real dollars by 2020, consuming 21 percent of GDP in the U.S. and 16 percent of GDP in other developed countries. There is no way we can afford this. We are a developing country and should focus on making money first, not spending it.

Great Debates

The Hippocratic Oath

Hand out copies of this pledge that all doctors are supposed to take and discuss the meaning of it.

I swear to fulfill, to the best of my ability and judgment, this covenant:

I will respect the hard-won scientific gains of those physicians in whose steps I walk, and gladly share such knowledge as is mine with those who are to follow.

I will apply, for the benefit of the sick, all measures that are required, avoiding those twin traps of overtreatment and therapeutic nihilism.

I will remember that there is art to medicine as well as science, and that warmth, sympathy, and understanding may outweigh the surgeon's knife or the chemist's drug.

I will not be ashamed to say "I know not", nor will I fail to call in my colleagues when the skills of another are needed for a patient's recovery.

I will respect the privacy of my patients, for their problems are not disclosed to me that the world may know. Most especially must I tread with care in matters of life and death. If it is given to me to save a life, all thanks. But it may also be within my power to take a life; this awesome responsibility must be faced with great humbleness and awareness of my own frailty. Above all, I must not play at God.

I will remember that I do not treat a fever chart, a cancerous growth, but a sick human being, whose illness may affect the person's family and economic stability. My responsibility includes these related problems, if I am to care adequately for the sick.

I will prevent disease whenever I can, for prevention is preferable to cure.

I will remember that I remain a member of society with special obligations to all my fellow human beings, those sound of mind and body as well as the infirm.

If I do not violate this oath, may I enjoy life and art, be respected while I live and remembered with affection thereafter. May I always act so as to preserve the finest traditions of my calling and may I long experience the joy of healing those who seek my help.

Vocab Refresh

Healthcare provider – a clinic, hospital, doctor or nurse.

Lower life expectancy – a statistic often used to measure standard of living in different countries.

Higher infant mortality – ditto.

The profit motive – a principle of self interest which states that entrepreneurs will only invest in a market where money is to be made, which ironically benefits society – not least through goods, services, innovation and jobs.

GDP – national income. The value of all goods & services produced by a country in a year.

Basic human right – something a person is entitled to just because they live. Particularly relevant in the founding of the United States and the United Nations.

Insurance premiums – monthly payments which cover the cost of an accident or emergency.

From cradle to grave – slogan of the early proponents of the British National Health Service.

Disability – an affliction which prevents a person from leading a normal active and working life.

Handicapped – a person with a permanent physical or mental disability, requiring special care.

Overblown bureaucracy – undesirable situation where an organization is dominated and weighed down by arguably unnecessary rules and rule-makers.

Unresponsive services – do not meet the needs of the people who wish to use them.

Government handout – a subsidy or benefits payment granted by the state.

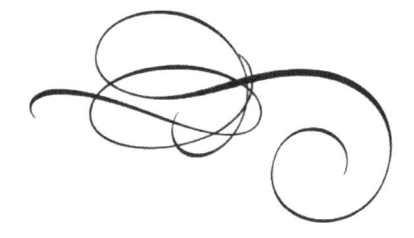

Debate 7 – Globalization

Debate 7 – Globalization

Should multinational companies or humanity benefit most from globalization?

Goals of the Lesson

- For students to become more familiar with the concepts and ethical questions of globalization.
- For students to practice debating, using persuasive devices and functional phrases.
- For students to find some form of consensus on the issue.

Rhetoric

Discuss and demonstrate these figures of speech with the class and explain that people who are able to speak forcefully and persuasively often use devices like this. Tell the students that you would like them to try and use these devices during the debate.

1. **Apostrophe** – where the speaker breaks off from the audience and talks to an imaginary person or abstraction.

'O Romeo, Romeo! wherefore art thou Romeo?' ~ Shakespeare, *Romeo and Juliet*

2. **Apposition** – the placing of two elements side by side, in which the second defines the first.

'An appositive, a grammatically incomplete noun phrase, is sometimes set off by commas, a reader-friendly invention.'

3. **Archaism** – use of an obsolete, archaic word. That is, a word or words used in olden language, e.g. Shakespeare's language.

'With this ring I thee wed.'

Logical Fallacies

The Logical Fallacy is a rhetorical device which has no grounding in actual fact and is used by people to unfairly gain the upper hand in debates. Being able to spot such a flaw goes a long way to invalidating an opponent's argument.

1. **Argument by Selective Observation** – aka cherry-picking. The positive aspects of your argument are emphasized but the negatives are conveniently omitted. Such one-sidedness goes hand in hand with the manipulation of statistics. See also **special pleading**.

'Technology brings happiness.'

2. **Argument by Selective Reading** – making it seem as if the weakest of an opponent's arguments was the best he had.

3. **Argument by Slogan** – using clichés to appeal to populist emotions.

'I'll support women's rights when they start buying the drinks.' ~ Don Lindsay, *A List of Fallacious Arguments*

Preamble

Globalization refers to the integration of national economies into the international economy through trade, foreign direct investment, capital flows, migration, and the spread of technology. Globalization is an unstoppable process, despite opposition among certain groups in the developed world, nobody in China or India is even questioning whether it is going to happen. Every year China and India together produce more graduates than the whole European Union.

The oldest form of international trade was the Silk Road which flourished throughout ancient history up until medieval times. Since then, nations that have been economically pre-eminent in the world have usually pushed for free trade. Proponents of free trade were Britain and the Netherlands in the 18th and 19th centuries, then the United States in the 20th century. Now China is now pushing for free trade of its exports across the globe and the breaking down of tariffs and other trade barriers.

1. <u>The Positives for Developed Countries</u>

- Cheaper natural resources and more access to source goods and services.
- Cheaper labour resources & loose labour laws (more intellectual capital available – talent & ideas).
- New markets to sell into.
- Lack of law in areas like environmental control and trade restrictions.
- Cheaper products for consumers.
- Travel and migration – new opportunities.
- Westernization – the spread of western values (e.g. law, lifestyle, technology, politics, language).

2. <u>The Negatives for Developed Countries</u>

- Outsourcing means loss of jobs in industrialized countries.
- Loss of competitiveness – once notable national players are losing their dominance.
- Devastated communities who were reliant on the old *status quo* of heavy industry.
- Immigration – making it more difficult to find work and business opportunities.
- Trade deficits – imports greater than exports.

3. The Positives for Developing Countries

- Outsourcing means more jobs – higher paid jobs.
- More information, communication & technology – computers, fiber-optics, science, hi-tech engineering.
- Booming industries in Asia and Eastern Europe (e.g. construction, manufacturing, IT, services).
- Travel and migration possible.
- New opportunities for the many.
- Westernization – the spread of western values (e.g. law, lifestyle, technology, politics, language).

4. The Negatives for Developing Countries

- Once notable regional players are now engulfed by multinational giants.
- Sweatshops
- Pollution
- Urbanization – crowded cities with slums.
- Loss of national sovereignty – Third World governments at the mercy of MNCs and other states.
- Westernization – the spread of western values (e.g. law, lifestyle, technology, politics, language).
- Loss of talent and ideas – brain drain of brightest individuals.

Debating Phrases

If you want to win arguments in formal situations use Latin phrases. *Caveat*: don't use them too much!

1. **Quid Pro Quo** [kwɪd proʊ kwoʊ] – 'You scratch my back, I'll scratch yours.

'The US are dealing with North Korea on a *quid pro quo* basis.'

2. **Per se** [pɜːseɪ] – 'as such'.

'I'm not saying he's stupid, *per se*, he just doesn't understand my point.'

3. **Ad hoc** [æd hɒk] – 'case by case'.

'You can't impose a foreign policy on the whole world. International relations should be decided on an ad hoc basis.'

Marco Polo Sets Sail from Venice (1430)

This picture from a 15th century manuscript in the Bodleian Library, Oxford, shows the departure of Marco Polo on his 24-year long journey through the Orient. He is one of the first Western people of note to traverse the Silk Road and he wrote about it in astonishing detail. Marco Polo and his family were traders based out of Venice, the most prosperous and populous city in Europe during the 13th century. The equivalent contemporary Chinese city was Hangzhou which had a population of 2.5 million. This dwarfed Venice by a factor of ten. From Polo's writing we can see that China boasted a far greater developments in terms of civilization and technology.

The Silk Road is the world's oldest example of transnational business, having been the primary conduit for exchange of goods and culture between East and West since Roman times. The route functioned until the age of European maritime expansion, which represented the first wave of truly global trade.

Great Debates

MNCs should benefit the most from globalization.

- MNCs give people jobs that they otherwise wouldn't have. It has to be a top-down process. MNCs create wealth, plus they pay people higher wages than they had before. If we limit the behaviour of MNCs then there would be no jobs at all. MNCs provide supply chain stimulation and benefit the local economy. This is called the trickle down effect. Meanwhile, the work forces in Western countries should keep updating their work skills. Making themselves more adaptable will keep them more employable.

- MNCs represent progress and modernity. They bring technology, they build houses and roads. The Third World would live in abject poverty without their generosity and the opportunity they provide. Without MNCs, peasants would be slaves tied to the land for generation after generation. The real unfairness is trying to limit the freedom of businesses and meddling in their markets.

- Economic decision-making is best left to corporations, not governments. It's more natural to just leave resources to allocate themselves. The market might have winners and losers in the short term but in the long term world-society will prosper with as few restrictions on trade as possible. Any schoolboy can tell you that there is no such thing as a level playing field. Trying to create one with unequal rules, regulation and handicapping is unnatural and inefficient. Governments should let companies do what they do best: provide jobs and make money.

- Globalization is inevitable so there is no way of making it serve specific goals. We are powerless to stop the flow of capital across borders and we should not try to fight it. Instead we should try to work within the system. Capitalism has been around for hundreds of years and we know it works. Let it be. The first stage of globalization has to be market (supply) led before the second stage can be politically driven to emphasize the importance of world citizens. Right now we are still in the first stage and we will be for the next 50-100 years.

- The companies are doing everyone a favour by promoting the Western lifestyle. They are bringing the Third World into the 21st century and we should thank them for it. In the future, everyone can wear Rolexes and eat burgers. Capitalism is a system that does more to bring people out of poverty than anything else. What's the alternative? Cleaning toilets for your whole life?

- Globalization already serves humanity pretty well. Goods are cheaper and more available. Even working class people in the Western world can enjoy many luxuries like travel and high-tech goods thanks to globalization. It will not take long time before everyone else catches up. Nowadays anyone who is bright and willing to work hard can enjoy such a standard of living. The world is a much fairer place than it has ever been. People in poor countries do not question the opportunity they have been given. It is only moaning liberals in the West who complain about globalization.

Humanity should benefit the most from globalization.

- The profits from MNCs go into the pockets of bosses and shareholders in rich countries and humanity gains nothing. MNCs are responsible for running sweatshops, paying the lowest possible wages and taking advantage of loose laws. If nobody stops the corporations, they will use all the natural resources, there will be nowhere nice to live, no trees, filthy rivers, etc. The whole world cannot have the same lifestyle as Americans, because in a finite world it will only lead to misery.

- MNCs should distribute their products in developing markets at lower prices so more people have access to them. Corporate imperialism must be stopped from completely taking over. Obscene profits should be redistributed to stakeholders and the wider community. Western governments and Third World governments should force them to do so. That is their responsibility. In a world economy, the wealth should be redistributed for the same reasons as it is at national level.

- MNCs must be controlled because they are greedy, profiteering and exploitative by nature. MNC managers and directors sit around in boardrooms plotting and scheming how to manipulate people and governments. They are bloodsuckers. If profits of private companies are so important we should make crack legal and allow dumping of toxic by-products into local rivers and streams.

- Outsourcing means millions of laid-off workers in developed countries. These people need to be protected. Is it more important for CEOs to save money and throw people into poverty than prevent the total collapse of industrial America? Also many countries produce such cheap goods that they dump them in Western countries to put the local companies out of business. Chinese companies flood markets with cheap, low quality goods and we can't compete. This is not fair trade and must stop.

- The main export of poor countries is usually agricultural goods. It is difficult for them to compete with stronger countries who subsidize their farmers. Because the farmers in the poor countries cannot compete, they are forced to sell their crops at a much lower price than what the market is paying. This is wasteful and unfair. We need a level playing field right now! MNCs take natural resources and give little in return. Humanity should have ownership and control over such important things.

- Globalization is inevitable and if it does not benefit humanity, it cannot occur. Communications, information and the English language are already being democratized. Globalization benefits humanity hugely because wars are less likely to happen. If two countries are part of the same supply chain, they are not going to fight each other because they will not want to give up their wealth. This is why the EU was founded. Empowerment and equality creates peace and understanding among peoples. This should be the primary reason for globalization.

A Win-Win Deal

Tell the students that there are four reasons people become involved in conflict: need, desire, concern and fear. If you can focus on **relationships** to address these factors, then you can engineer a win-win situation where everyone benefits.

Split the class into two groups.

The first group is Blue Chip Inc. They are a rich technology company and prefer to build their computers and mobile phones in Third World countries. They choose to do business in these places because the nations there often have large, underemployed workforces and are frankly desperate for any sort of investment. This means Blue Chip can save fortunes and keep their shareholders happy. As well as this, they avoid a lot of bureaucracy and unnecessary regulations. They believe they are helping these poor countries get richer.

The second group is a human rights organization and NGO. They think Blue Chip are exploiting these poor countries and they want to see them pay higher wages and make their workers work fewer hours. as well as introduce new benefits. They think Blue Chip are guilty of modern day slavery and corruption. If Blue Chip do not agree, they will start a campaign in the media to embarrass them and lobby the government to crack down on them. They also think that because Blue Chip have so many overseas subsidiaries, they should be investigated for tax evasion.

Hash out an argument and agreement between the two organizations. They should start by setting out their position and then later on move to the haggling stage.

Vocab Refresh

MNC – Multinational Company, sometimes known as a transnational company.

Stakeholder – a party who affects, or can be affected by, the company's actions. That is, not just employees, owners and mangers, but the local community, society, government, suppliers, creditors, customers and shareholders.

Profiteering – seeking or exacting exorbitant profits, esp. through the sale of scarce or rationed goods.

Exploitative – to use selfishly for one's own ends.

Subsidize – to give aid in the form of payments to an industry or company. A semi-legal form of bribery.

Abject poverty – complete and miserable poverty.

Moaning liberals – a complainer with liberal views, 'liberal' meaning: maximum individual freedom possible, as guaranteed by law and secured by governmental protection, restriction of aristocracy, open-minded, etc.

Handicapping – to place a person at a disadvantage purposely to give the others a chance.

Blue chips – multinational companies.

The trickle-down effect – allowing the wealth in a country to reach the masses via tax cuts for the wealthy. See Debate 5.

Obscene profits – disgustingly high levels of profit, often accrued among an environment of shortage.

Inevitable – unstoppable.

Democratized – made accessible to the main population.

Empowerment – giving people confidence, a voice and opportunity to achieve their goals.

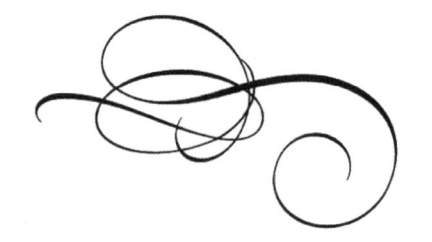

Debate 8 – Drugs

Debate 8 – Drugs

Should drugs be legalized?

Goals of the Lesson

- For students to become more familiar with the arguments for and against drug legalization.
- For students to practice debating, using persuasive devices and functional phrases.
- For students to find some form of consensus on the issue.

Rhetoric

Discuss and demonstrate these figures of speech with the class and explain that people who are able to speak forcefully and persuasively often use devices like this. Tell the students that you would like them to try and use these devices during the debate.

1. **Assonance** – the repetition of vowel sounds, most commonly within a short passage of verse.

'That solitude which suits abstruser musings' ~ Samuel Taylor Coleridge, *Frost at Midnight*
[*Abstruse* = hard to understand / esoteric]

2. **Asteismus** – facetious or mocking answer that plays on a word

Benedick: God keep your ladyship still in that mind! [of not marrying] so some gentleman or other shall scape a predestinate scratch'd face.
Beatrice: Scratching could not make it worse, an 't were such a face as yours were.
Benedick: Well, you are a rare parrot-teacher.
Beatrice: A bird of my tongue is better than a beast of yours.
~ Shakespeare, *Much Ado About Nothing*

3. **Asyndeton** – omission of conjunctions between related clauses.

'I came, I saw, I conquered.' ~ Julius Caesar

Logical Fallacies

The Logical Fallacy is a rhetorical device which has no grounding in actual fact and is used by people to unfairly gain the upper hand in debates. Being able to spot such a flaw goes a long way to invalidating an opponent's argument.

1. **Argument from Authority** – claims that the speaker is more of an expert than his or her opponent and is by implication, correct. Similar to **appeal to authority**.

'You get bad decisions and good ones. Believe me, it does even itself out.' ~ Alex Ferguson

2. **Argument from False Authority** – a humble variation on the above. A bit of patronizing false modesty.

'I'm not a doctor but ….'

3. **Argument from Small Numbers** – over-generalizing based on a small sample.

'My Granddad smoked two packs a day all his life and he lived to 93.'

'I've thrown three sevens in a row. Tonight I can't lose.' ~ Carl Sagan, *The Fine Art of Baloney Detection*

Preamble

Adapted from Wikipedia.

Illegal drugs include:

- Crack – freebase cocaine, stimulant, highly addictive.
- Cocaine – powdered extract of the coca plant, stimulant, habit forming.
- Heroin – derivate of the opium poppy, relaxant, painkiller, highly addictive.
- LSD – hallucinogen, subjects the user to trips lasting a few hours. Can be psychologically damaging.
- Ecstasy – tablet form of chemical MDMA. Love drug with retroactive side-effects on central nervous system.
- Weed – relaxant, subjects the user to improved mood and heightened senses. Little or no side effects.
- Speed – stimulant, addictive with adverse 'comedown'.
- Crystal Meth - similar effects to speed.
- Anabolic Steroids – growth hormone used for muscle building. Adversely effect reproductive system.

The Netherlands has operated a pragmatic policy of drug tolerance and non-enforcement of drug laws. Most policymakers in believe that if a problem has proved to be unsolvable, it is better to try controlling it instead of continuing to enforce laws with mixed results.

By contrast, most other countries take the point of view that drugs are detrimental to society and must therefore be outlawed, even when such policies fail to eliminate drug use. Consequently the Dutch government spends a lot on treatment, education, harm reduction, and health research. As a consequence of this liberalism, the Netherlands is a major transit point for drugs entering Europe and the country is a major producer, distributor and consumer of illicit drugs.

In the Netherlands 9.7% of young adults (aged 15-24) consume soft drugs once a month, comparable to the level in Italy (10.9%) and Germany (9.9%) and less than in the UK (15.8%) and Spain (16.4%), but much higher than in, for example, Sweden (3%), Finland or Greece. Dutch rates of drug use are lower than U.S. rates in every category.

US States have periodically adopted what is known as 'Zero Tolerance' policies on drugs. Under the 1973 Rockefeller drug laws, the penalty for selling two ounces or more of heroin, morphine, opium, cocaine, or cannabis, including marijuana (these latter two being removed a few years later), or possessing four ounces or more of the same substances, carried a sentence the same as that for second-degree murder: a minimum of 15 years to life in prison, and a maximum of 25 years to life in prison.

However, this did not stop the whole country experiencing a massive crack epidemic that lasted throughout the 1980s. The greatest social costs of crack were associated with prohibition-related violence. Research suggests that crack was the most prominent factor contributing to the rise and fall of social ills in the African American and Latino communities between 1980 and 2000.

> 'Between 1984 and 1994, the homicide rate for black males aged 14 to 17 more than doubled, and the homicide rate for black males aged 18 to 24 increased nearly as much. During this period, the black community also experienced an increase in fetal death rates, low birth-weight babies, weapons arrests, and the number of children in foster care.' – Steven Levitt

> 'As a result of the low-skill levels and minimal initial resource outlay required to sell crack, systemic violence flourished as a growing army of young, enthusiastic inner-city crack sellers attempt to defend their economic investment.' – James Inciardi, 1994

The European Monitoring Centre for Drugs and Drug Addiction (EMCDDA) noted in its 2001 report in a chapter on problem drug use – defined as injecting drug use and/or long-duration/regular use of opiates, cocaine and/or amphetamines – that "countries with more liberal drug policies (such as the Netherlands) and those with a more restrictive approach (such as Sweden) have not very different prevalence rates, the impact of national drug policies on the prevalence of drug use and especially problem drug use remains unclear."

Debating Phrases

If you want to win arguments in formal situations, use Latin phrases. *Caveat*: don't use them too much!

1. **De facto** [deɪ ˈfæk toʊ] – 'unofficial' – in actual fact / in practice.

'Although they are not recognized by the UN, Kosovo enjoys *de facto* independence from Serbia.'

2. **Ergo** [ˈɜr goʊ] – 'therefore'

'The pirates who invaded this fort left Sparrow locked in his cell; ergo, they are not his allies.' ~ *Pirates of the Caribbean*

3. **Et cetera** [ɛt ˈsɛt ər ə] – 'and the rest', 'and so on' or 'and more'.

'We, Nicholas II, By the Grace of God, Emperor and Autocrat of All the Russias, King of Poland, Grand Duke of Finland, et cetera, et cetera, et cetera.'

The House of the Poppy Merchant – George Barbier (1924)

This print captures the decadent spirit of the roaring 20s. The drug was glamourized by high society in Europe since the publication of *Confessions of an English Opium Eater* a century earlier. This spirit somewhat declined with the demise of colonialism. One might suggest that the reality of opium addiction is somewhat removed from this nature of portrayal in art and literature.

Chez la Marchande de Pavots.

Yes, drugs should be legalized.

- If drugs are legal then users will no longer visit dangerous criminal dealers. If we can take their main income away, they will not be so powerful. Soft drugs like cannabis do less harm than the crime that prohibition creates. Illegal drugs mean large profits and this is socially and ethically wrong.

- Because of the huge profits involved with illegal drugs, they create violence, corruption and political and economic destabilization. Just look at Afghanistan, Latin America, the Caribbean and Southeast Asia. These regions are unsafe, violent; they breed terrorists and dictatorships that profit from drugs while the majority of the people suffer in poverty.

- If we make drugs illegal we can control the ingredients. One of the biggest dangers of drugs is that nobody knows what chemicals are really in them. Illegal drugs are very impure and dangerous. We can prevent unnecessary deaths, especially by providing clean needles. Prevention is better than cure. This has worked really well in Holland and has saved the government money in health spending.

- Legalization means there will be less theft, robbery and murder to obtain them. Legalization will make our streets safer. Addicts can be monitored and receive help. Not just go underground. Everyone is not going to suddenly become drug addicts – we have jobs, families and responsibilities. It is the economy (lack of jobs) that causes crime rates among the youth, not drugs. Banning drugs doesn't work either – people who want them will always find a way to get them – it's already a big market.

- The government can tax drugs. The money from this can be spent on addiction recovery and clinics to help people. If alcohol and tobacco were discovered today they would be banned immediately. However, as it is the government make billions of dollars in tax revenue from these two drugs. Legalization is clearly a positive move.

- Many illegal drugs have fewer health dangers than alcohol and tobacco. In the UK there are 40 million social drinkers, 11 million are 'at risk' or 'problem' drinkers, and 9 million smoke cigarettes. 500,000 people take ecstasy every weekend resulting in 40 deaths a year. Meanwhile there are 6500 deaths due to alcohol and 120 000 deaths from smoking, making the risk of ecstasy half that of alcohol, and well below tobacco.

- Some drugs can be used for medicine and comfort. Ecstasy helps with people with Parkinson's disease and people suffering from post-traumatic stress disorder, such as people who have been raped. Cannabis can be used for chemotherapy MS and AIDS patients. It increases their appetite and counters nausea.

- What people do in private should not be regulated by the government. It's their body, as long as they are not doing harm to others, what is the problem? What right does the government have to stop an individual harming himself? The government does not forbid overeating, which causes a lot more deaths every year.

Great Debates

No, drugs should not be legalized.

- Legalization will make drugs cheaper. That means people will take more drugs, more people will take drugs, younger people will take drugs and there will be more profits for dealers. We will develop a culture of drug taking and society will suffer because drugs destroy people's mental and physical health. The bottom line is that drugs wreck families.

- Prohibition works. The police and government should copy Rudy Giuliani's 'Zero Tolerance' policy that worked in New York. This policy of harsh crackdowns on all forms of crime helped to eliminate the 1980s crack epidemic. Drugs are such a big threat to society that only severe penalties will work. China has strong anti-drugs laws and they do not have a problem with drugs.

- If the government allows soft drugs like cannabis to be legal, then teenagers and other people will graduate on to harder drugs. Soft drugs are a gateway to hard drugs such as heroin. This is because kids come into contact with dealers and other people who take drugs. They get used to breaking the law so they think it's normal. Then they try harder drugs to get a better 'high'.

- Few things restrict people's freedom as much as violence, drugs and crime in society. If we refuse to take responsibility and fail to ban drugs, the market will be gifted to organized criminals. Crime, violence and drug use go hand in hand. In the US, six times as many murders are committed by people under the influence of drugs, as by those who are looking for money to buy drugs.

- Drugs are bad for people's health. Not only are they naturally harmful but they spread disease through sharing needles. Any doctor will tell you that drugs are much more deadly than alcohol. Alcohol is used by seven times as many people as drugs but the number of deaths caused by those substances is not far apart.
  Drug deaths 15,800, alcohol deaths 18,500 – Centre for Disease Control & Prevention (2000).

- Drugs make people become losers in life. Drugs also harm other people because users treat their friends and family badly. If everyone does drugs then society will be less productive. We need to keep drugs illegal to protect our children. Drugs cause schizophrenia and many other health problems.

- Legalization is really promoting drug use. Why don't we legalize murder, and robbery, and all the other crimes, and then we won't have a crime problem. Legalizing drugs would send the wrong message to our children. We already have enough problems with alcohol and tobacco in our society – why should we add to it?

- Legalization would not stop crime. People would just find other ways to make money. We already have a black market in cigarettes and alcohol and these are legal. If the government tried to tax drugs, people would simply buy their drugs from the black market.

Binge Drinking

Discuss the phenomenon of binge drinking. What are the problems associated with it? Why do people do it? Where is it most common? Who drinks the most? How much a binge? Mention that the word binge originally mention to soak something in liquid – i.e. clothes. The word 'bender' also has an interesting origin meaning to spend a whole sixpence (which could be bent) on a bout of several days' drinking away from home.

Ask students to search for the most recent internet article or forum thread that they can find on the topic of drunkenness, binge drinking or alcohol in society. Each student should post a relevant comment on the discussion. The comment should be around two paragraphs in length and should express an clear opinion.

Vocab Refresh

Destabilization – To undermine the power of (a government or leader) by subversive or terrorist acts.

Prohibition – to ban something from public consumption.

Legalization – to make something legal. A step up from decriminalization.

Obtain – to get / receive usually through some sort of endeavor.

It counters nausea – nausea is a feeling of uneasiness / sickness.

Zero tolerance – a policy of disproportionately severe penalties for crimes.

Harsh crackdowns - the severe or stern enforcement of regulations, laws, etc., as to root out abuses or correct a problem.

The 1980s crack epidemic – a craze for crack smoking which swept through America as imports of cheap cocaine freebase flooded into Florida and California from Latin America.

Severe penalties – [self explanatory].

Restrict people's freedom – consider the freedom paradox: the first sign of a civilized society is the rule of law, i.e. the restriction of freedom.

Under the influence – mentally impaired due to the use of drink or drugs.

Black market – contrast with 'grey areas'.

Schizophrenia – a severe mental disorder characterized by emotional blunting, intellectual deterioration, social isolation, disorganized speech and behaviour, delusions, and hallucinations.

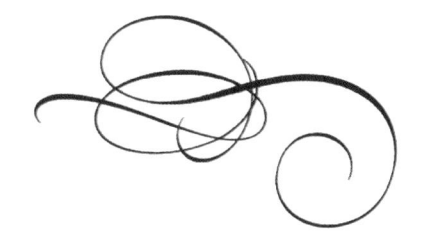

Debate 9 – Tax

Debate 9 – Tax

Do Rich People Pay Too Much Tax?

Goals of the Lesson

- For students to become more familiar with the concepts and ethical basis of taxation.
- For students to practice debating, using persuasive devices and functional phrases.
- For students to find some form of consensus on the issue.

Rhetoric

Discuss and demonstrate these figures of speech with the class and explain that people who are able to speak forcefully and persuasively often use devices like this. Tell the students that you would like them to try and use these devices during the debate.

1. **Allegory** – an extended **metaphor** in which a story is told to illustrate an important attribute of the subject.

E.g. *Aesop's Fables.*

2. **Alliteration** – a series of words that begin with the same letter or sound alike.

'Buxom British beauty bowls over Bollywood by baring body in bra' ~ headline from *The Sun*.

3. **Allusion** – an indirect reference to another work of literature or art.

'I violated the Noah rule: predicting rain doesn't count; building arks does.' ~ Warren Buffett

Logical Fallacies

The Logical Fallacy is a rhetorical device which has no grounding in actual fact and is used by people to unfairly gain the upper hand in debates. Being able to spot such a flaw goes a long way to invalidating an opponent's argument.

1. **Ad Hominem** – attacking the person rather than the argument.

Bill	I believe that abortion is morally wrong.
Dave	Of course you would say that, you're a priest.
Bill	What about the arguments I gave to support my position?
Dave	Those don't count. Like I said, you're a priest, so you have to say that abortion is wrong. Further, you are just a lackey to the Pope, so I can't believe what you say.

~ from Nizkor.org

2. **Affirming the Consequent** – logic reversal – a statement of the form 'if P then Q' gets turned into 'Q therefore P'.

If I have the flu, then I have a sore throat.
I have a sore throat.
Therefore, I have the flu.

3. **Ambiguous Assertion** – a statement is sufficiently unclear that it leaves some sort of leeway. Similar to **equivocation**.

'Last night I shot a burglar in my pyjamas.'

Preamble

Taxation is a necessary duty for every responsible citizen of a country. It is required to fund public services such as schools, hospitals and the police force as well as to provide benefits to the weaker members of society. In this way taxation is a tool for redistributing the wealth of society, to level the playing field as it were. This is known as the 'Robin Hood Effect' because he was said to have stolen from the rich to give to the poor.

The idea that rich people should pay a higher percentage of tax than poorer folk is called **Progressive Taxation**. A **Regressive Tax** is where poor pay a higher proportion of their income than the rich, e.g. a flat rate tax.

Examples

1. **Income tax** (progressive) – In the year 10, Emperor Wang Mang of China instituted an unprecedented tax – the income tax – at a rate of 10 percent of profits for professionals and skilled labour. (Previously, all Chinese taxes were either head tax or property tax).

2. A true progressive income tax was first implemented in Britain by William Pitt the Younger in his budget of December 1798 to pay for the looming Napoleonic Wars. Today, the middle rate of income tax in the UK (for salaries of £35,000 – £150,000) is 40% and above that it is 50%. The basic rate for everyone else is 20%.

3. **Corporation tax** (progressive) – a tax levied on the net income (profits) of companies. In the US this is levied at 35% for profits over $18.3 million while it can be as low as 15% for companies with income of under $50,000. Ireland has the lowest corporate tax rate in the developed world at 12.5%. Obviously the burden of corporation tax lies with the wealthy owners of firms.

4. **Sales Tax** (similar to VAT) (regressive) – levied when a commodity is sold to its final consumer. This is a 'pay for what you spend tax' in which rich and poor pay an equal rate. Rich people therefore spend a small proportion of their income on sales tax. Thus, food, utilities and other necessities are usually exempt since poor people spend a higher proportion of their incomes on these commodities.

5. **Poll Tax** (regressive) – a *per capita* or 'soul tax' levied as a set amount on every individual. The introduction of a poll tax in medieval England was the primary cause of the 1381 Peasants' Revolt, and in 1990 Margaret Thatcher's introduction of the Poll Tax caused widespread civil

unrest and refusal to pay by poor people who were taxed a relatively large proportion of their income.

6. **Capital Gains & Inheritance Tax** (progressive) – e.g. the tax on the profits made form the sale of shares and other unearned wealth. Obviously rich people have a much higher burden in these taxes than poor people.

7. **Customs Duty** (regressive) – E.g. tariffs on goods brought into a country. Buying cigarettes, alcohol, perfume or jewellery in airports is always cheaper because they are sold beyond international jurisdictions, without duty.

8. **Environment Tax** (regressive) – e.g. road tolls such as the congestion charge in London. Ecotaxes tend to put a burden on consumption, affecting poor more than rich.

Debating Phrases

Stipulate that the teams must use these phrases.

Ways to open a debate

1. We would like to begin by issuing the following statement.
2. We believe it is necessary to ….
3. We would like to introduce our position by giving the following statement.
4. We would like to outline the main features of this problem, firstly ….
5. In the first place we would like to make clear that ….
6. The main argument focuses on ….

Death and the Miser – Hieronymus Bosch (1494)

This painting shows Death coming for the Miser, who is actually poor in the fact that he lives a spartan existence and has no friends or family around him. But ignorant of his fate, he is still foolishly fixated by worldly goods as the demon tempts him with a bag of money. In the foreground, the Miser is shown in good health, hoarding his tainted wealth next to his bed for no good reason.

Great Debates

No, rich people do not pay too much tax.

- Progressive taxation is fair because the duke can afford more than the dustman. It would be totally unfair if the dustman had to pay the same percentage of tax as the duke. The rich are able to contribute something more than everyone else and so it is not unreasonable that they should.

- All human beings need a certain amount of money to live on. For poor people this amount is a large part of their income, while for rich people this amount is a small piece of theirs. Excess wealth therefore should be used and not hoarded. Because poor people have a shortage, they need assistance from the government so they can survive. This is not unreasonable.

- In most western European countries and the United States, most economists and social scientists support progressive taxation. They realize that completely proportional taxation is not even a possibility. In the U.S., the vast majority of economists (81 percent) support progressive taxation. Even economists as far removed as Adam Smith and Karl Marx argued in favour of progressive tax.

- Inequality in taxation creates equality in a wider, more important sense: equality in life and opportunity. This builds a stronger, fairer society where the poor are given an advantage in life to allow them to contribute what they are truly capable of. This is why some countries are developed and 'civilized' while are others are not. There is a good reason why Robin Hood (an outlaw) is admired in world culture.

- Those who control great amounts of capital within a society, generally participate more directly in shaping government policy, often in ways that further maximize their wealth. Thus, it is a natural fact that the wealthiest in a society will, on average, become even disproportionately wealthier over time. This causes long term political instability as the working class gets ever larger and a super-rich elite become even more powerful.

- A progressive tax is an automatic stabilizer. If a person suffers a decrease in wages, for example due to a recession, then the money regained by being in a lower tax bracket lessens this blow.

- Rich people are not going to get any sympathy from me by whining that their huge salaries aren't as huge as they could have been, because some of it is being used for public good. The wealthy have a far greater interest in public goods and services such as defence, security of property rights and infrastructure than the poor since they have more to lose when these goods / services fail.

- The rich are pretty good at dodging tax by using international tax havens and other methods of concealment and deception. In the UK more than 100,000 people who earn over £10 million a year – including super-rich foreign owners of football clubs, do not pay any income tax at all.

Yes, the rich pay too much tax.

- High tax on the rich is bad for the economy because it discourages investment and spending which in turn slows down job creation, which in turn leads to unemployment. This then leads to drops in tax revenue and increased welfare spending which in turn leads to even higher taxes on the rich.

- The Brain Drain. High progressive taxes may encourage emigration because taxes are not the same in every country. Very high earners are able to relocate in order to pay less tax. Emigration only increases with rises in the top rates of tax. The difference in the higher rates of tax between the United States and Europe helped to cause the brain drain of high-earners to America in the 1960s. The UK experienced a brain drain to the US, Hong Kong, Australia and other countries in the late 1970s when the top rate on earned income was 83% and the rate on unearned income was 78%.

- Tax avoidance. During times of high taxation, high earners often find tax havens (self-governed offshore islands with banking secrecy and low taxation) to protect their income. Tax *evasion* is also widespread yet it is difficult to stop or catch offenders.

- High taxes cause an increase in tax loopholes such as "income splitting" techniques. High taxes create an incentive for business owners to split their business into smaller, less efficient ones for a lower tax rate. It also encourages production from less efficient smaller businesses than larger ones.

- While the top 5 percent of rich people in most countries pay over half the taxes, they only have 5 percent of the voting weight. Furthermore, if tax is to be progressive, surely it should mean a greater say in elections for those who contribute the most.

- Progressive taxes mean there is less incentive to work. If someone pays half his income in taxes, he has no reason to try to increase his or her income above the base level. He may as well take a lower-paid but easier job and make the same money.

- Policymakers are under pressure from lower and middle income voters to limit higher incomes through progressive taxes. This is corrupt and unfair. Progressive taxation breaks the idea of equality under the law. This is the idea that each individual is subject to the same laws, with no person, group or class having special legal privileges.

The National Budget

Tell the students that the UK government income from taxation is nearly £600 billion per year. However, their spending is usually well over that. 2008 figures: £575bn vs £618 bn.

Give each student an imaginary £600 billion and ask them to make a list – in order of priority – of which areas they think the money should be spent on. Then ask them to make a new list guessing roughly what *percentage* of the revenue should be spent on each area.

The actual breakdown for the UK looks something like this.

Social protection	28 %
Health	19 %
Housing & environment	4 %
Defence	5 %
Education	13 %
Public order & safety	5 %
Industry, agriculture, employment and training	3 %
Transport	3 %
Interest on debt	5 %
Other spending	15 %

Vocab Refresh

Progressive taxation - rich people should pay a higher percentage of tax than poorer folk.

Infrastructure - the fundamental facilities and systems serving a country, city, or area, such as transportation and communication systems, power plants, and schools.

Disproportionately wealthy – the irony of people who are embarrassingly rich while being surrounded by a community that is desperately poor.

Whining – synonym of moaning, whingeing or excessive complaining in annoying and shrill tone.

Dodging tax – slangy term for avoiding tax. Dodge = to duck.

Incentive – a reason do something, often money. A big juicy carrot at the end of a stick.

The Brain Drain – a phenomenon where many of the bright people in a region migrate to where the economic climate is more favourable.

Income inequality – uneven distribution of wealth within a society.

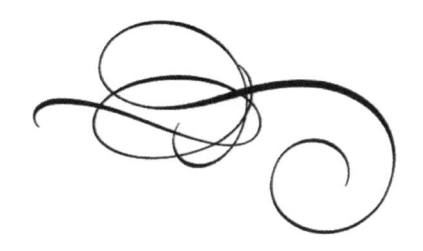

Debate 10 – Friends & Enemies

Debate 10 – Friends & Enemies

Is the enemy of your enemy your friend?

Goals of the Lesson

- For students to become more familiar with the concepts of international relations.
- For students to practice debating, using persuasive devices and functional phrases.
- For students to find some form of consensus on the issue.

Rhetoric

Discuss and demonstrate these figures of speech with the class and explain that people who are able to speak forcefully and persuasively often use devices like this. Tell the students that you would like them to try and use these devices during the debate.

1. **Auxesis** – a form of **hyperbole**, in which a more important sounding word is used in place of a more descriptive term.

A lawyer may refer to a scratch as a 'wound' or 'laceration.' ~ *Webster's*

2. **Bathos** – deliberately bad or mock poetry caused by an incongruous combination of high-brow and low-brow forms designed to give comedic effect. Similar to **anticlimax**.

'The ballerina rose gracefully en pointe and extended one slender leg behind her, like a dog at a fire hydrant.' ~ Jennifer Hart

3. **Cacophony** – the juxtaposition of words producing a harsh sound.

'We want no parlay with you and your grisly gang who work your wicked will.' ~ Winston Churchill

Logical Fallacies

The Logical Fallacy is a rhetorical device which has no grounding in actual fact and is used by people to unfairly gain the upper hand in debates. Being able to spot such a flaw goes a long way to invalidating an opponent's argument.

1. **Argument from Spurious Similarity** – a bad analogy. Similar to **false cause**.

"Italy, cradle of the Roman Empire and later founder-nation of both fascism and the shoe industry is shaped like a boot. Australia, leading light of the Southern hemisphere and dogged participant in both World Wars, looks like the noble head of a Scottish terrier. And, of course, the UK, birthplace of the world's largest empire, is shaped like a giant witch with a pig under her arm. If we allowed the great China's chicken's wings and tail to be clipped, how could we hope to succeed as a nation?" ~ Lu Penghuai, Chinese minister

2. **Begging the Question** – assuming the answer, reasoning in a circle, **tautology**. The thing to be proved is used as one of your assumptions.

'Paranormal phenomena exist because I have had experiences that can only be described as paranormal.' ~ Bob Carroll, *The Skeptic's Dictionary*

3. **Black and White Rather than Shades of Grey** – or seeing two ends of the spectrum as the same. Such absolutism often arises through wishful thinking or ignorance, rather than deliberate deception.

'Everyone is imperfect' – Mohandas Gandhi was imperfect and Joseph Stalin was imperfect, but they were not the same shade of imperfection. ~ Eliezer Yudkowsky, *Lesswrong.com*

'Either the nobles of this country appear wealthy, in which case they can be taxed for good; or they appear poor, in which case they are living frugally and must have immense savings, which can be taxed for good.' ~ John Morton, Archbishop of Canterbury from 1486 to 1500. This over-simplification is known as **Morton's Fork**.

Preamble

From Wikipedia.

The phrase, 'the enemy of my enemy is my friend' is usually considered a foreign policy doctrine that is commonly used to confront a significant enemy through an intermediary in order to undermine the enemy and in a 'cold' manner, as opposed to a 'hot', direct confrontation. It's an ancient proverb that means that solely because two parties have a common enemy, they are friends. Often described as an Arab proverb, there is also an identical Chinese saying and both may be an extension of another Chinese proverb that says, 'It is good to strike the serpent's head with your enemy's hand.' A historical example of this policy occurred when the Greeks were attacked by the Persians at Thermopylae; the Greek city states put aside their differences and fought the common enemy.

'Divide and Rule' was the overarching foreign policy of the Roman Empire and in a later age, of the British Empire especially in India. The Romans and in particular Caesar would go into a new territory and immediately befriend the weakest tribe and whomever else was willing to form an alliance. This would usually create a division of loyalties in the region which is what Caesar wanted. He would then proceed to attack the strongest of his enemies, one by one until every tribe had been toppled or surrendered and thus forced under the protection of the Roman People. Caesar knew that if all of the foreign tribes were allowed to unite in confederacy against the common enemy of Rome, they would be much harder to beat so he purposely engineered divisions among populations of foreign countries like Gaul in order to keep them weak and in a state of perpetual distrust with one another.

After the defeat of Napoleon in 1805, Great Britain held the balance of power in Europe for the next century, and had the responsibility of maintaining order and peace on the continent through a system of alliances. This meant that an increase in strength of one state would be kept in check by a corresponding increase in strength of their geographic or political enemy. The belief was that this would prevent war and it led to nations entering into unlikely alliances in order to maintain the system. With Italy and Germany consolidating into large states towards the end of the century, the balance of power changed dramatically which led Britain and France themselves enter into fateful military agreement against Germany and the Austro Hungarian Empire. The ramifications of this ratcheting up of nationalistic fervor and promises of support led to the greatest carnage in the history of warfare, the First World War (1914-1918).

The geopolitical makeup of the Middle East demonstrates some clear examples of the policy of befriending your enemies' enemies. Saddam Hussein was openly backed by the UK & US during the Iran–Iraq War, despite being at extreme odds ideologically with British and American notions of liberal democracy. This particular hypocritical and interventionist policy goes back to the 19th century when Iran was the regional superpower and allied to Britain who competed against Russia for influence over the Persian kings or Shahs. Around the turn of the century when oil was first being produced, the Iranians fell out with Britain and refused to sell them oil. Britain subsequently drew up the boundaries of a new state on Persia's doorstep to counterbalance Persia's influence in the region. Iraq therefore, is essentially a Western fabrication combining three disparate peoples: the Kurds, the Sunnis and the Shias. This is created an adversary of Iran and thus a friend of Britain and America. Britain and the US have also continually supported oppressive regimes in Saudi Arabia in order to provide a check on Iran's hegemonistic aspirations and ensure stability in the region whilst protecting the flow of oil to Western markets.

Since WWII the US had traditionally adopted a realistic approach to dealing with regimes of contrasting ideologies in order to achieve strategic regional aims. During the Cold War both the Soviet Union and the US built up a network of alliances and vassals throughout the world in the attempt to indirectly challenge each other's ideology and socio-economic system. The Iran–Contra affair, doing business with and indeed backing tyrants like Saddam Hussein, Robert Mugabe, Osama bin Laden, Augusto Pinochet, Suharto and apartheid South Africa was all par for the course of 1980s US foreign policy. But the question is, does this policy of pragmatism really work?

Debating Phrases

<u>English Legal Concepts</u>

Burden of proof – the necessity of proof lies with the complainer. Innocent until proven guilty, etc.

Absolute power – 'Power corrupts and absolute power corrupts absolutely.' ~ William Pitt

Conflict of interest – when someone has an interest that might influence their reliability. Impropriety that can undermine confidence.

Abuse of power – 'With great power comes great responsibility.' ~ FDR

Victor's justice – The winner makes the rules – actually a fundamental concept in the UN charter.

Balance of power – a doctrine intended to prevent any one nation from becoming sufficiently strong so as to enable it to enforce its will upon the rest. Equilibrium between competing nations.

Battle of the Virginia Capes – V. Zveg (1962)

During the American War of Independence, the French joined forces with the American Colonists both on land and at sea to expel the British Army from the continent. The French played a particularly important role in tipping the balance and displayed a high degree of support and co-operation. However, the French and Americans culturally and linguistically are not natural allies. Even to this day, the relationship is often a strained one with sporadic misunderstandings between the people and governments of the two the nations.

The Battle of the Chesapeake took place in 1781 and is a classic of naval warfare, pitting two great commanders – Hood and de Grasse – against each other. The French fleet on the left, outnumbered the British. The battle itself was a draw but it allowed the landing of troops on the continent while cutting off British reinforcements. Thus it directly led to the final defeat of Cornwallis at Yorktown.

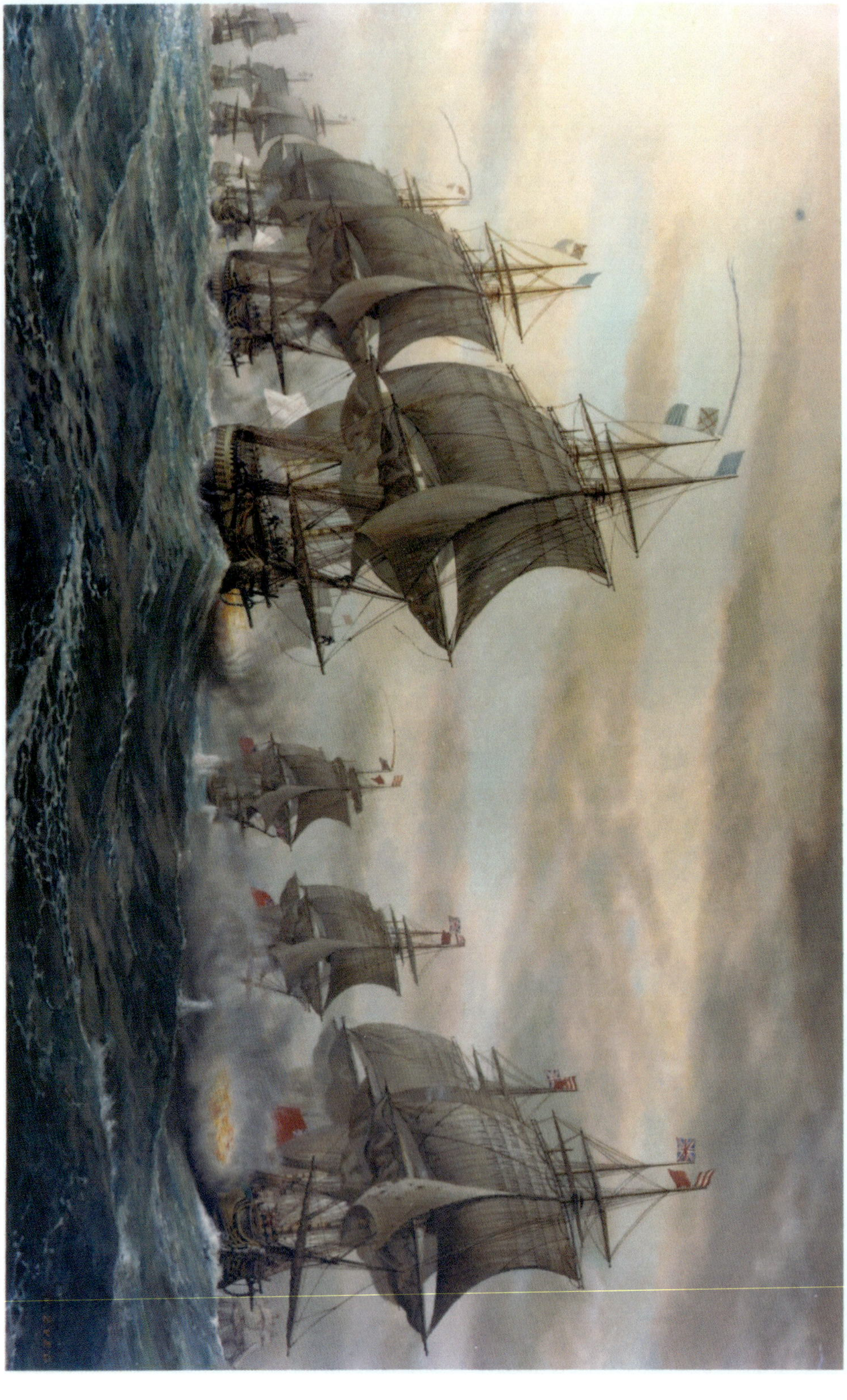

Yes, the enemy of my enemy is my friend.

- The Pilot Fish cleans parasites off larger predators like sharks. These smaller fish swim freely around the sharks and even inside the mouths of the sharks that could easily eat the small fish. Since the shark's enemy is the parasite and the parasite's enemy is the smaller fish, the shark considers the Pilot Fish a 'friend' and accommodates an otherwise potential food source.

- Pragmatism is best because it works. In this world, only the strongest and smartest can survive. Being too principled makes you inflexible. If you lose the war or get invaded because you failed to play the political game – you are a bad leader and your people will hate you. Your country will be poor and your people will be slaves.

- The end justifies the means. Power is more important than ideology. Reality is more important than idealism. We don't live in an ideal world, so we have to make the best of a bad situation and that means doing business with people we don't like, to defeat a greater enemy. This is logical thinking.

- Nietzsche said 'The best weapon against an enemy is another enemy'. The nice guy is a loser. If you are nice to everyone and you don't use the resources available to (i.e. your enemies' enemies) then you will be beaten and it will be your own fault. History punishes those who do not prepare and think ahead. A government must use all the options available to make sure the country is as safe as possible.

- Nietzsche also said 'The man of knowledge must be able not only to love his enemies but also to hate his friends.' Friends can become enemies very easily because circumstances change. Margaret Thatcher said: 'It pays to know the enemy – not least because at some time you may have the opportunity to turn him into a friend.'

- People say a country who practices this are hypocrites and untrustworthy, but this is a *tu quoque* fallacy (a 'you too' argument, similar to *ad hominem*). Yes, the West is morally bankrupt but that does not mean its enemies are any less bad. Just because America has done some bad things does not mean they should allow other people to do bad things. Saying we can not have an opinion because of what we did before is foolish.

- The country being 'manipulated' should be thankful it has a powerful protector. If the bigger country did not offer support it would be swallowed up by the common enemy. The policy is a very practical one that benefits both sides. We would not have won the Second World War if the Allied powers (Britain, France, America, Russia and China) did not put aside their differences and fight the common enemy (the Axis powers). The policy saved the world.

Great Debates

No, the enemy of my enemy is not necessarily my friend.

- Using your enemy's enemy as an ally is problematic because there is probably very little other common ground. If the common enemy disappears the friends might turn on each other. The US backed militia in Afghanistan fighting the USSR but then the Taliban became the USA's greatest enemy. During WWII the differences between the Allies and the USSR were not important because they had a common enemy. But after the war there were decades of far more dangerous threats between the two.

- The relationship between friends and enemies is not black-and-white. Both being against one thing does not mean they are both for the same things. Good people don't make enemies easily so do you really want to be doing business with a person who openly has enemies and probably has many others? This kind of temporary 'friend' is unlikely to be a true friend.

- The idea is hypocritical. People should live by their principles not change their friends at the drop of a hat. If you don't have principles you have no integrity therefore you cannot be trusted. Making shallow short-term alliances is not a good recipe for success in life or in the world. Good people don't befriend someone unless they agree on many things and see the world in very similar ways. They don't make friends just to attack someone else. That's a short-sighted and dishonest strategy.

- If countries like America want the world to respect them, they should behave in a way that shows they are true to their beliefs and morals. If America pretends to the world that it loves freedom and democracy but it supports cruel dictators, how can we trust America? This is true for any country, not just America. You must be true to yourself.

- Britain and America are morally bankrupt. They make friends with bad people when it suits them and attack when times change. It's all about money and resources. It is dangerous to ask for help from these countries because they will control you. Who wants to live in a dog-eat-dog world?

- In the long term the policy can't work. America shot themselves in the foot by supporting bin Laden. With the internet, globalization and the war on terror, this policy is more dangerous than ever because small isolated groups can link up with other extremists to cause trouble. The big western powers cannot really do that as efficiently to defeat them. These days you beat your enemy by superior, more ethical ideas and a superior social system, not by double dealing and unlikely friendships that can easily fall apart and backfire.

Great Debates

Global Hegemony

Ask students to research and write an op-ed piece for a newspaper about one of the following topics:

1. How long do most empires last?
2. Why do empires collapse?
3. How much longer has America got as top dog in the world?
4. How long will China have at the top?
5. How will Chinese dominance be different from American power?

Some things to consider:

1. The ancient empires ruled for thousands of years. The Romans, 500 years. The British, two-hundred.
2. Technology. Empires usually rise and fall because people get access to an innovation and it becomes widespread, whether it be a pike, a vessel, a loom, steam engine or bomb.
3. If we can extrapolate based on the pattern in point 1 then it looks like America may have as little as fifty more years at the top.
4. Arguably the world is so flat and 'democratized' now that China couldn't steal a march on anyone for that long.
5. The two are very different countries yet share some similarities. If you look at it historically, America arguably has a worse human rights record than China. Slavery, annihilation of the native people and expansionist wars for resources are all examples of this. China doesn't have a notable religious side to it's culture either.

Vocab Refresh

Hypocrite – a person who pretends to have virtues, moral or religious beliefs, principles, etc. Someone who says one thing and does the opposite.

At the drop of a hat – do something quickly and easily, without thinking about it.

Integrity – adherence to moral and ethical principles; soundness of moral character; honesty.

Morally bankrupt – being in a position where you have done so many bad things, you cannot take the moral high ground any longer. It would be extremely hypocritical to do so.

Shot themselves in the foot – to do something with the intention if it benefiting yourself but in reality is has the opposite effect. Similar to '**backfire**'.

Parasite – an organism that lives on or in an organism of another species.

Pragmatism – character or conduct that emphasizes practicality above theoretical concerns.

The end justifies the means – a rather cynical phrase meaning, do whatever is necessary even if it is morally wrong, in order to achieve a morally right result.

Ideology – a body of beliefs and doctrine that underlie a system.

Nietzsche – a 'trendy' 19th century German philosopher with some profound but odd ideas.

Manipulate – to use someone to your advantage without them knowing it.

Dog-eat-dog world – a tough and overly competitive society.

Ethical – honest and fair.

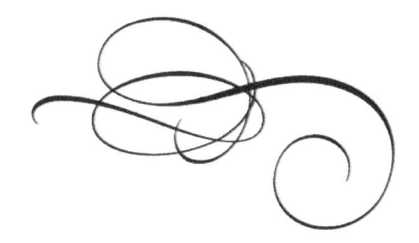

Debate 11 – Contribution to Society

Debate 11 – Contribution to Society

'From each according to his ability to each according to his need' – Is this fundamentally a good idea?

Goals of the Lesson

- For students to become more familiar with the concept of economic production in society
- For students to practice debating, using persuasive devices and functional phrases
- For students to find some form of consensus on the issue

Rhetoric

Discuss and demonstrate these figures of speech with the class and explain that people who are able to speak forcefully and persuasively often use devices like this. Tell the students that you would like them to try and use these devices during the debate.

1. **Catachresis** – a **mixed metaphor** or the use of wrong words; sometimes used by design and sometimes a rhetorical fault. Similar to **malapropism**.

'Can't you hear that? Are you blind?'

2. **Chiasmus** – two or more clauses related to each other through a reversal of structures in order to make a larger point. Also known as **antimetabole**.

'I have taken more out of alcohol than alcohol has taken out of me.' ~ Winston Churchill

3. **Circumlocution** – talking around a topic by substituting or adding words, as in **euphemism** or **periphrasis**.

E.g. any dictionary definition or euphemism.

Logical Fallacies

The Logical Fallacy is a rhetorical device which has no grounding in actual fact and is used by people to unfairly gain the upper hand in debates. Being able to spot such a flaw goes a long way to invalidating an opponent's argument.

1. **Burden Of Proof** – if you can't disprove it, I must win by default.

Bill   I think that some people have psychic powers.
Dave   What is your proof?
Bill   No one has been able to prove that people do not have psychic powers.
~ from Nizkor.org

2. **Causal Reductionism** – *reductio ad absurdum* – oversimplification or exaggeration. Trying to use one cause to explain something, when in fact it had several causes. Einstein's constraints is useful here: "Everything should be made as simple as possible, but no simpler."

'The nation's current lack of moral standards was caused by the poor example set by Bill Clinton when he was president.'

'Taxation is theft.'

N.B. *Reductio ad absurdum* is can be a fair way and effective to argue, if the cause is clear and true.

3. **Equivocation** – using a word to mean two different things.

'The sign said 'fine for parking here', and since it was fine, I parked there.'

Preamble

From Wikipedia.

Under a communist system, every person should contribute to society to the best of their ability and consume from society in proportion to their needs, regardless of how much they have contributed. In the Marxist view, such an arrangement will be made possible by the abundance of goods and services that a developed communist society will produce; the idea is that there will be enough to satisfy everyone's needs.

Is this thinking still relevant today? Could a wealthy and functioning society possibly work on this principle with everybody being paid the same salary and an absence of luxury goods and services? Many would argue from the 'greed is good' Adam Smith perspective which states that society as a whole prospers because the individual is selfish. Not selfish in a bad way, merely self-interested in that the butcher does not give you a pound of meat just because he is generous. He is doing it because he is thinking, 'Great, here's another customer and another £3.50 in my pocket.' The fact that we have food on our table every evening is thanks to someone else's self interest. This is a fundamental precept of the market and humans have functioned this way since the inception of civilization.

In the founding of the American colonies, Captain John Smith famously ordered his wastrel countrymen: 'He who does not work shall not eat.' which actually first appears in the Bible (II Thessalonians 3:10). This encouraged the early Jamestown colonists to pull together and function as a group instead of a rag tag bunch of individuals. Vladimir Lenin later adopted this motto as one of the founding principles of communism but did not aim it at lazy people, rather the bourgeois owners of capital who lived off the labour of others.

The debate today really boils down to whether the group is more important than the individual and whether the individual should work for the benefit of the group which includes the weakest members of society or should he produce for himself, allowing the fruits of his toil to indirectly trickle down to the rest in a more Darwinist way.

Debating Phrases

<u>Addressing the House</u>

- I request the floor
- I wish to have the floor.
- I rise to a point of information / point of order.
- I wish to speak in favour of / against this motion / resolution / amendment because ….
- Is the Chair / the speaker (not) aware that ….

Detroit Industry, North Wall – Diego Rivera (1932)

This fresco was painted during the Great Depression and depicts the harmony and fruits that can be achieved through combined labour. It is part of a collection of similar murals which display strong religious and marxist themes. Detroit is a mid-western city famed for being the epicenter of the American automotive industry, in particular the Ford Motor Company which pioneered mass production several years before the painting of this piece.

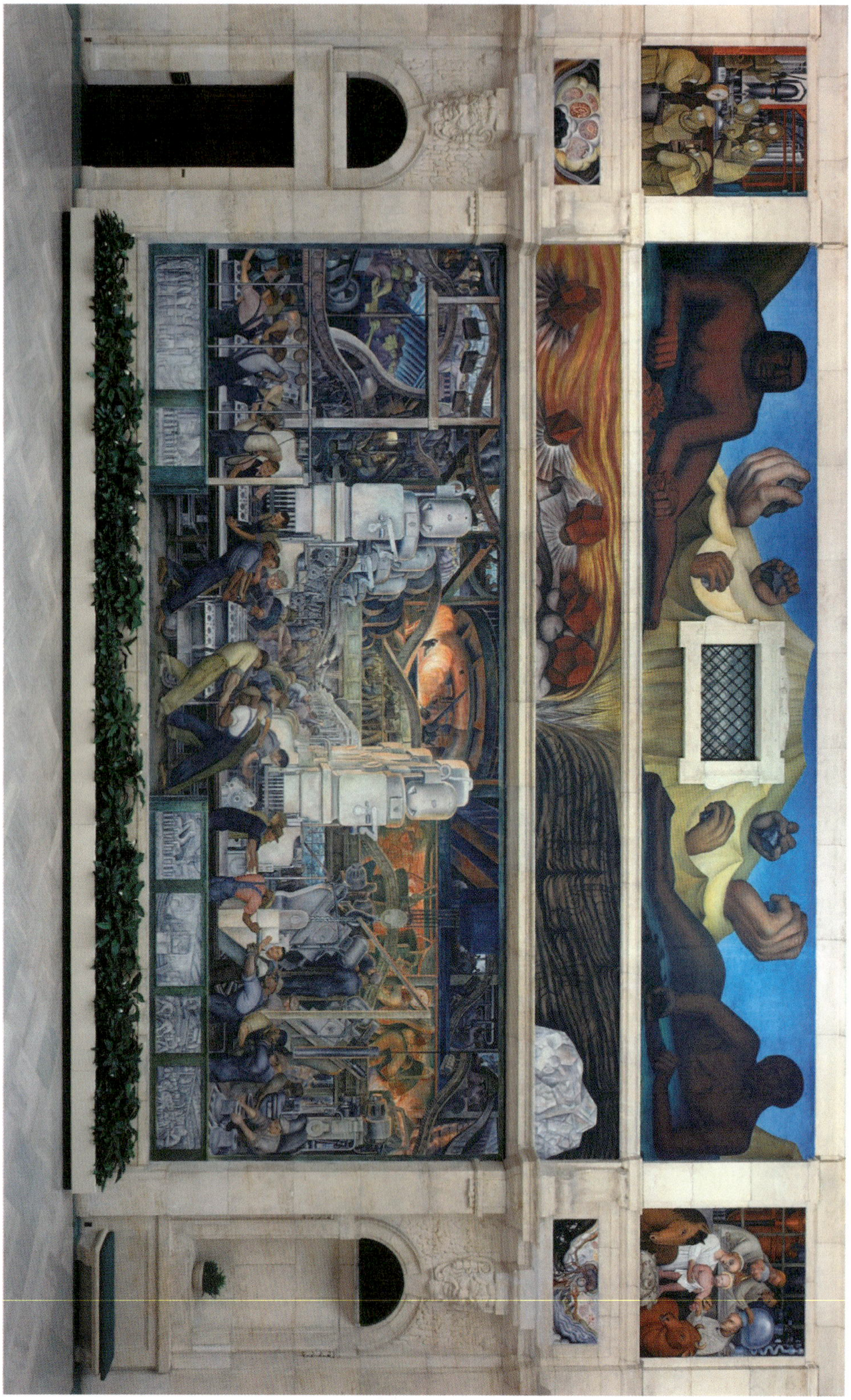

Yes, from each according to his ability to each according to his need is a good idea.

- It would be better if people were motivated to work for the good of society, not just for their own personal ends. It would create a society of caring people not just money-grubbing self-centered individuals. This would be a step forward in human evolution. Everyone has a right to a basic standard of living, even if they are unable to earn it by their own efforts.

- It would better if low paid workers were not so unfairly rewarded for their hard labour while the business owners do very little in terms of physical work yet get more than they need. It addresses unfairness in society. *'He who does not work shall not eat.'* Lazy bosses who just play golf and sit in leather chairs and count their profits all day should have to work like everyone else. Rich people just live off the labour of others.

- It means that poor people won't have to pay very high prices for goods by buying things on credit. Society is pushed to consume more and more but this spending just gets everyone in debt. This was the cause of the 2008 financial crisis. It would be better if we only consumed what we needed and didn't live beyond our means. Social problems like alcoholism and gambling typically hurt the poor. These can be eliminated because they are wasteful.

- Open Source software is a clear example of people with ability giving the product of their talents to those who need it, for the greater good of society. Open source products are a wonderful way to empower the disadvantaged people of the world. For world society to prosper, ownership and ideas should be in the public domain. We need more philanthropy. All the big companies in the world could easily give their products to the poorest people in the world for free. Why don't they want to make the world a better place? It would profit everyone in the long run.

- The more productive or most talented workers can support the weaker if profits are shared, just as parents must by law, provide for their children. People would be more encouraged to do work that suits them rather than just go for the money. The type of work is more important to your happiness than the material results of your work.

- The welfare state is fundamentally a fair idea. In a world society the policy of each according to his need, regardless of his ability, would level the playing field for everyone. Everyone has a right to a basic standard of living, even if they are unable to earn it by their own efforts. Thus, for example, the able-bodied are morally bound to subsidies the handicapped.

- It may not be possible in our current system, but it makes perfect sense that everybody does what they can, and gets what they need – it's just plain old efficiency. The super-rich pay very little tax and their money is hoarded. This is a disgusting waste of resources. For world society to prosper, every person should be equal.

No, from each according to his ability to each according to his need is a bad idea.

- Talented people would not be rewarded individually therefore it is difficult for a society to prosper. Creative industries like fashion, art, music and other service industries cannot spring up so easily because they provide a luxury (non-essential) product. Therefore society as a whole suffers. Plus, if you create something like a song or a book and cannot profit from it personally, then what is the point in creating it at all? Society will suffer from such a policy. We will go back to the Dark Ages.

- If there's no personal reward for creating new things then there's no incentive to strive. People will become lazy. People will refuse to forge ahead, refuse to push the limits of human ingenuity because there's no profit motive for them to do so. Profits are also necessary because they go into R&D to improve the next generation of products, science and technology for all mankind. Innovation needs a profit motive.

- It's a breach of personal freedom – freedom to make and keep money, freedom to create and choose, freedom to pursue happiness and take risks. Plus, there will always be a black market for luxuries, people will find a way to produce and get things they wish for. You cannot kill the market – it's as natural as evolution. 60 percent+ of the world population are greedy. Humans as a species are not suited to communism.

- It can only work on a small scale. Such thinking implies forced sharing (government forced), which many object to. You would have to convince the rich to give up their wealth, and they would rightly turn round and say 'No I worked for it'. For those who are happy to work and contribute you would have those who are unwilling to do so and expect the state to provide for them.

- It is a nice thought but impossible to enforce in practice. Nice idea, wrong species. It requires more trust than the free market. Frank Zappa said: 'Communism will never work because people like to own stuff'. Churchill said: 'The inherent vice of capitalism is the unequal sharing of blessings; the inherent virtue of socialism is the equal sharing of miseries.'

- It drags the best people down to the same level as everyone else. There is no free lunch in this world. Those who are willing to work hard and use their talents should be rewarded. Why should we support the lazy ones? People who believe in 'each according to his need' are envious of people who have more than they do.

What's Your Business Idea?

Ask the students to think of business idea and create a sales pitch to convince investors to buy into the scheme. Spend sometime brainstorming and encouraging entrepreneurial zeal. Each student should present his or her idea to the class and field questions on the viability of the idea.

Vocab Refresh

Fundamentally – being an essential part of, a foundation or basis; basic, underlying.

Money-grubbing – overly greedy, materialistic, bottom-line focused.

Open Source – an approach to design, development, and distribution of a product by offering public accessibility and peer-based collaboration.

Live beyond your means – to spend more money than you earn or are capable of earning.

Philanthropy – large scale charity on the part of wealthy individuals' or organizations.

Level the playing field – create an equal footing for all, democratizing opportunity.

Morally bound – forced by rules of right conduct.

Plain old efficiency – plain old refers to common sense wholesome ideas, time-tested.

The Dark Ages – a period of intellectual regression after the fall of the Roman Empire.

Incentive to strive – incentive being an attractive reason to do something.

To forge ahead – to get stuck into to new work, possibly while others are hesitating.

Human ingenuity – the ability of humans to solve almost any problem.

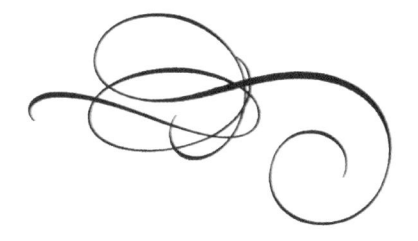

Debate 12 – Free Trade

Debate 12 – Free Trade

Is protectionism sometimes necessary in trade?

Goals of the Lesson

- For students to become more familiar with the concepts and economics of free trade.
- For students to practice debating, using persuasive devices and functional phrases.
- For students to find some form of consensus on the issue.

Rhetoric

Discuss and demonstrate these figures of speech with the class and explain that people who are able to speak forcefully and persuasively often use devices like this. Tell the students that you would like them to try and use these devices during the debate.

1. **Classification** – linking a proper noun and a common noun with an article.

'Elvis the popstar.'

2. **Climax** – the arrangement of words in order of increasing importance.

'… the unalienable rights of life, liberty, and the pursuit of happiness.' ~ Martin Luther King

3. **Consonance** – the repetition of consonant sounds, most commonly within a short passage of verse.

'Pitter patter'

Logical Fallacies

The Logical Fallacy is a rhetorical device which has no grounding in actual fact and is used by people to unfairly gain the upper hand in debates. Being able to spot such a flaw goes a long way to invalidating an opponent's argument.

1. **Error of Fact** – beyond plain ignorance this is often a form of intellectual dishonesty caused by lack of rigorous due diligence in ensuring the truthfulness of the position.

'No one knows how old the Pyramids of Egypt are.' – Except, of course, for the historians who've read the records written by the ancient Egyptians themselves.

2. **Euphemism** – the attempt to make the content emotionally palatable with the consequence of making the meaning less precise.

The term 'developing countries' rather than 'poor countries'.

3. **Exception That Proves the Rule** – this is used when a rule has been asserted, and someone points out the rule doesn't always work. This is usually a fine argument, however, many people think that this cliché somehow allows you to ignore the exception altogether.

Preamble

Protectionism is the economic policy of restraining trade between nations through methods such as:

- **Tariffs** – a tax on imported good to increase the cost to importers, and increase the price of imported goods in the local markets, thus lowering the quantity of goods imported. Tariffs may also be imposed on exports.

- **Quotas** – reduce the quantity of a certain type of good entering a market, and therefore increase the market price of that good.

- **Subsidies** – government payments / loans to help out struggling industries and give them an advantage over foreign competitors and protect local jobs.

- **Legislation** – food safety regulations, environmental standards, labour laws, complex certification procedures and anti-dumping bills can do a lot to stop foreign products coming in.

- **Exchange rate manipulation** – a government may intervene in the foreign exchange market to lower the value of its currency by selling it. Doing so will raise the cost of imports and lower the cost of exports.

These measures are designed to discourage imports and prevent foreign take-over of local markets and companies. This policy is closely aligned with anti-globalization, and contrasts with free trade; where government barriers are kept to a minimum.

This is what Adam Smith had to say about protectionism in *The Wealth of Nations*:

> The natural advantages which one country has over another in producing particular commodities are sometimes so great that it is acknowledged by all the world to be in vain to struggle with them. By means of glasses, hotbeds, and hot walls, very good grapes can be raised in Scotland, and very good wine too can be made of them at about thirty times the expense for which at least equally good can be brought from foreign countries. Would it be a reasonable law to prohibit the importation of all foreign wines merely to encourage the making of claret and burgundy in Scotland? But if there would be a manifest absurdity in turning towards any employment thirty times more of the capital and industry of the country than would be necessary to purchase from foreign countries an

equal quantity of the commodities wanted, there must be an absurdity, though not altogether so glaring, yet exactly of the same kind, in turning towards any such employment a thirtieth, or even a three-hundredth part more of either. Whether the advantages which one country has over another be natural or acquired is in this respect of no consequence. As long as the one country has those advantages, and the other wants them, it will always be more advantageous for the latter rather to buy of the former than to make. It is an acquired advantage only, which one artificer has over his neighbour, who exercises another trade; and yet they both find it more advantageous to buy of one another than to make what does not belong to their particular trades.

This thinking heavily influenced British politics, famously with the repeal of the Corn Laws in 1846. The Corn Laws were tariffs designed to protect British wheat from cheap foreign imports. The abolition of these laws was a significant step turning Britain from a mercantilist to a free trade economy. The problem was however, that when famine struck Ireland in 1845, there was actually plenty of corn but it was all being sold to England because of the repeal and because the Irish peasants had no money to buy it. This was compounded with the next Liberal government in England refusing to intervene or provide aid, believing Irish wealth should relieve Irish poverty. Thus out of a population of 8.5 million, 2 million died and 2 million emigrated thanks to the *laissez faire* doctrine of Smith.

Worsening the Great Depression

Protectionism is seen as one of the follies of government policy during the Depression Era. Because demand for goods and services in the US evaporated, the government introduced prohibitive tariffs on imports into the United States. Foreign trade at the time was a small part of American economy and mostly limited to agriculture, but to Europe trade with the US represented a much larger share of their total economic activity. When the US imposed 50% tariffs (up from 25.9%) the rest of the world responded with retaliatory tariffs causing a vicious cycle of economic contraction globally. After the Depression, many governments were forced to move to the extreme right or left due to social upheaval, leading to World War 2.

Debating Phrases

Addressing the House

- Does the speaker (not) agree with me that ….
- The speaker stated in his speech …. Does he (not) realize that ….
- I yield the floor (to points of information).
- I urge the house to give me its support by voting for / against this motion / resolution / amendment.

The Destruction of Tea at Boston Harbor – Nathaniel Currier (1846)

The Boston Tea Party is a good example of how protectionism can backfire. The British imposed a tariff on the tea they wished to sell in the American colonies, which infuriated the people and led to revolution. The British government at the time was in need of revenues to fight wars in Asia and they were also angered by the smuggling of tea into the colonies. Smuggling was widespread and indeed a big enterprise on both sides of the Atlantic.

Great Debates

"THE DESTRUCTION OF TEA AT BOSTON HARBOR."

Yes, protectionism is sometimes necessary in trade.

- Domestic companies and industries are destroyed by free trade. They have their profits and market share reduced by cheaper imported goods. Foreign competition leads to job losses at home. Margaret Thatcher's free trade policy caused the closure of 80 percent of the coal mines in England and Wales and devastated whole communities. Free trade encourages dumping. That is, when a country supplies another with goods and below cost-price just for the purpose of wrecking their domestic industries.

- Protectionism has been used by every country which has become economically powerful. From the 1840s until World War 2, America had the highest industrial tariff rates in the world. After the War, Japan, Korea, Germany, France and the Scandinavian countries closed off their industries to foreign investment and set up state ownership in key industries. The Japanese car industry did not exit in the 1960s. They used tariffs to develop their own technology.

- Latin America was forced by the IMF to adopt liberal trade policies but performed poorly since tariff cuts in 1980s and 1990s, compared to protectionist China and Southeast Asia (4 Dragons) plus Japan. Greater harm comes from allowing big corporations to destroy a small local economy, than comes from putting restrictions on the free market. Since trade liberalization the annual GDP per capita growth of the developing world has been half what it was during the days of protectionism in the 1960s and 1970s.

- The arms, financial, media and energy industries get assistance and protection from the UK government. Politically important industries like defence cannot be allowed to fall into foreign hands or disappear altogether. All key industries in a country should be protected from foreign competition until they are able to compete globally, especially in fledgling economies. This includes: shipping, mining, textiles, steel, oil and gas, electronics, cars, banking. They should be nurtured and protected by tariffs, subsides, regulations etc. That's how South Korea, Germany, Japan and Taiwan got rich.

Great Debates

- Subsidies stimulate growth. Ireland has one of the highest standards of living in the world but 30 years ago it was an agricultural backwater with high unemployment. The Irish government used subsidies to turn the country into a high-tech economy. Trade barriers should help poor nations develop domestic industries – get through teething and reach a certain level of competence.

- Capital moves to the place of cheapest labour, where it exploits people. Sweatshop labour is often used by MNCs. Therefore the poor can become poorer under free trade as they are reduced to slavery. Also, laws should be in place to stop companies in rich countries from offshoring work and putting people out of jobs at home.

- Why should developed countries dictate to the poor countries what they can and can't sell? The developing countries like to dominate developing nations but won't let these same countries gain an advantage in trade. This is totally unfair and bad for the world.

No, free trade is best.

- Consumers gain from free trade. No restrictions on imports from foreign countries mean that consumers get more choice and cheaper stuff. Reduction in taxes / tariffs also stimulates economic growth for foreign companies and economies. This is good for the world economy and makes a richer, fairer and more peaceful world in the long term.

- Free Trade means unprofitable companies and industries go out of business and their capital goes towards more profitable enterprises and markets. In the long term the whole economy benefits by allowing foreign competition. Likewise, blocking free trade stifles the economy and protects loss-making businesses. Career change, retraining and finding a new job is difficult and risky for many people but it is worth it. No pain no gain.

- Protectionism harms the people it means to help because it makes the country less competitive in the long term. Protectionism is inefficient because it encourages production in non-profitable industries when that money could be invested in something more lucrative, stable or high-tech. Free Trade is more efficient. Protectionism is old fashioned and short-sighted.

- Alan Greenspan, former chairman of the US Federal Reserve, criticized protectionism because it leads to "a waste of our competitive ability. ... If the protectionist route is followed, newer, more efficient industries will have less scope to expand, and overall output and economic welfare will suffer." Protectionism in Europe and America caused the Great Depression to continue much longer than it should and it made it much worse. In the 1930s world trade dropped by 70 percent as countries blocked each others' goods in retaliation, while trying to save themselves.

- In poorer exporting countries, the growth of manufacturing and the many other jobs that the new export sector creates has a ripple effect throughout the economy. The growth creates competition among producers, lifting wages and living conditions. Also, workers in the Third World only accept jobs if they are the best on offer. If they accept low-paying jobs from western companies it shows that the jobs they would have had otherwise are even worse.

- Nearly all economists support free trade. Free trade creates more jobs than it destroys because it allows countries to concentrate production in goods and services that they have an advantage in. Often foreign governments subsidies their industries to gain an unfair advantage in overseas markets. Free Trade benefits both sides.

- Protectionism is one of the major causes of war. There was almost constant warfare in the 17th and 18th centuries among European countries whose governments were protectionist. The American Revolution happened because of British tariffs and taxes. Protective policies preceded World War 1 and 2. When goods cannot cross borders, armies will.

The Trading Game

The following game is adapted from the IMF website. Split the class into 6 teams representing Europe, Africa, Asia, North America, South America and Australia. Each team has the following commodities to trade.

Europe – $9,000, cheese 1,000kg, fish 2,500kg, shoes 200 pairs.
Africa – $2,000, cocoa 1,000kg, cotton 5,000kg, gold 10 oz.
Asia – $7,000, rice 10 tonnes, rubber 5 tonnes, steel 16 tonnes.
North America – $10,000, beef cattle 4,000lb, lumber 10,000 board feet, wheat 50 tonnes.
South America – $5,000, bananas 8 tonnes, coffee 2,000kg, crude oil 400 barrels.
Australia – $8,000, aluminium 5 tonnes, coal 100 tonnes, wool 800 kg.

Let the trading begin. For example, Africa must choose what they would like to buy. They decide on shoes from Europe. The Europeans make them an offer of say 25 pairs for $425. The Africans decide whether to accept the offer or ask for a cheaper price / different quantity. The teams should keep a record of their trades. The game can continue indefinitely. After several rounds of deal-making, see who has what and who has come out with the most money, and value for money.

If any of the teams begin to be left out because they wasted their resources early on, you can offer them a loan at fifty percent interest.

Vocab Refresh

State ownership in key industries – government ownership in strategically vital areas of production, paid for through taxation and nationalization.

The IMF – The International Monetary Fund give loans and assistance to struggling economies.

Trade liberalization – removal of tariffs and other protectionist measures.

GDP per capita growth – the increase in the average salaries of a population. Calculated as all the money produced in a country in a year, divided by the population.

Fledgling economies – countries experiencing rapid international trade gains, though have traditionally been poor, authoritarian and agricultural nations.

Putting restrictions on the free market – trying to limit the amount of trade with other countries through regulations, tariffs, currency manipulation, quotas, subsidies, etc.

Standard of living - the quality and quantity of goods and services available to people, and the way these goods and services are distributed within a population, usually measured by inflation, per capita income, life expectancy, educational standards, income equality, cars per household, tvs per household, quality of healthcare, etc.

Agricultural backwater – a remote, unsophisticated, backward place.

Teething – the first growth of teeth, metaphorically applied to emerging nations or organizations.

Sweatshop labour – a factory imposing Dickensian-style working conditions.

To offshore work – to contract out work overseas.

A ripple effect – a knock-on / domino effect.

Stifles the economy – chokes the economy.

Lucrative – highly profitable.

Retaliation – reciprocally punitive measures.

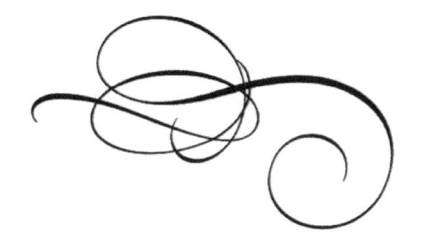

Debate 13 – Reciprocity

Great Debates

Debate 13 – Reciprocity

'An eye for an eye and a tooth for a tooth' – Is this a fair statement?

Goals of the Lesson

- For students to become more familiar with the ethical basis of justice and retribution.
- For students to practice debating, using persuasive devices and functional phrases.
- For students to find some form of consensus on the issue.

Rhetoric

Discuss and demonstrate these figures of speech with the class and explain that people who are able to speak forcefully and persuasively often use devices like this. Tell the students that you would like them to try and use these devices during the debate.

1. **Ellipsis** – omission of words.

'Wise men talk because they have something to say; fools, because they have to say something.' ~ Plato

2. **Enthymeme** – informal method of presenting a **syllogism** – an inference / supposition. Inductive reasoning.

'There is no law against composing music when one has no ideas whatsoever. The music of Wagner, therefore, is perfectly legal.' ~ Mark Twain

3. **Epanalepsis** – repetition of the initial word or words of a clause or sentence at the end of the clause or sentence.

'The king is dead, long live the king.'

Logical Fallacies

The Logical Fallacy is a rhetorical device which has no grounding in actual fact and is used by people to unfairly gain the upper hand in debates. Being able to spot such a flaw goes a long way to invalidating an opponent's argument.

1. **Extended Analogy** – reading too much into a similarity. Forcing the metaphor too much.

A person who advocates a particular position (say, about gun control) may be told that Hitler believed the same thing. The clear implication is that the position is somehow tainted. But Hitler also believed that window drapes should go all the way to the floor. Does that mean people with such drapes are monsters? ~ Don Lindsay, *A List of Fallacious Arguments*

2. **Failure to State** – if you just keep attacking your opponent but never actually outline your own opinion. Can easily lead to *ad hominem*.

3. **False Dichotomy** – assuming there are only two alternatives when in fact there are more. Similar to **black and white** thinking.

'Either you are with us, or you are with the terrorists.' ~ George W Bush

Preamble

From Wikipedia.

The phrase 'an eye for an eye and a tooth for a tooth' is a Hebrew expression which appears in the Book of Exodus in which a person who has taken the eye of another in a fight is instructed to give his own eye in compensation. At the root of the non-Biblical form of this principle is that one of the purposes of the law is to provide equitable retaliation for an offended party. It defined and restricted the extent of retaliation. This early belief of 'mirror punishment' or exact reciprocity is prominent in the laws of the Hebrew Bible. The Latin term for this concept is *lex talionis* and applies to legal systems that specify formulaic penalties for specific crimes, which are thought to be fitting in their severity.

Anglo-Saxon law substituted payment of wergild for direct retribution: a particular person's life had a fixed value, derived from his social position; any homicide was compensated by paying the appropriate wergild, regardless of intent. Under the British Common Law, successful plaintiffs were entitled to repayment equal to their loss (in monetary terms). In the modern law system, this has been extended to translate non-economic losses into money as well.

New laws developed as early civilizations grew and a less well-established system for retribution of wrongs, feuds and vendettas, threatened the social fabric. Despite having been replaced with newer modes of legal theory, *lex talionis* systems served a critical purpose in the development of social systems – the establishment of a body whose purpose was to enact the retaliation and ensure that this was the only punishment. This body was the state in one of its earliest forms.

It is surmised that in societies not bound by the rule of law, if a person was hurt, then the injured person (or their relative) would take vengeful retribution on the person who caused the injury. The retribution might be much worse than the crime, perhaps even death. Law put a limit on such actions, restricting the retribution to be no worse than the crime, as long as victim and offender occupied the same status in society, while punishments were less proportional with disputes between social strata: like blasphemy or *lese majeste* (against a god, viz., monarch, even today in certain societies), crimes against one's social better were systematically punished as worse.

Christian tradition differs somewhat from this concept, advocating 'turning the other cheek' following Jesus' Sermon on the Mount which focused on the importance of showing forgiveness to enemies and those who harm you. In Islam the Quran permits exact and equivalent retribution. The Quran, however, softens the law of an eye for an eye by urging mankind to accept less compensation than that inflicted upon him or her by a Muslim, or to forgive altogether.

Court orders Iranian man blinded – Friday, 28 November 2008

A court in Iran has ruled that a man who blinded a woman with acid after she spurned his marriage proposals will also be blinded with acid. The ruling was reported in Iranian newspapers on Thursday. The punishment is legal under the Islamic Sharia principle of qias, equivalence or analogy, which allows retribution for violent crimes. The court also ordered the attacker, 27-year-old Majid Movahedi, to pay compensation to the victim. The acid attack took place in 2004. The victim, Ameneh Bahrami, went to Spain for surgery to reconstruct her face but efforts to restore her sight failed. The ruling was a response to her plea to the court in the Iranian capital Tehran for retribution. "Ever since I was subject to acid being thrown on my face, I have a constant feeling of being in danger," she told the court. Ms Bahrami also said that Movahedi had also threatened to kill her.

news.bbc.co.uk/2/hi/middle_east/7754756.stm

Some alternative penalty systems exist which primarily concern the impact of the punishment on the sanctioned offender and/or on society, while demanding non-parallel penalties. For example the correctional prison system (first instituted in the USA in the early 20th century) is based on the idea that the purpose of law enforcement is to correct the deviant nature of criminals by compelling them to reflect and regret their crimes during a lengthy incarceration; another alternative, the reformatory, was invented to reform, i.e. re-educate, young offenders.

Critics maintain that merely limiting vengeance is not enough as even limited retaliation continues a potentially endless cycle of violence. Mahatma Gandhi remarked: 'An eye for an eye will make the whole world blind.' Other belief systems adhere to similar concepts, such as the Taoist *wúwéi* which encourages a wronged individual to simply accept the infraction and to take the least "resistive" action to correct it, if any action need to be taken at all. Buddhism stresses the weight of karma: one can take retributive action, but that retributive action is not without its consequences, and living on a finite planet guarantees that the suffering incurred by a retributive action will return to the individual who was wronged (as well as the one who did the wrong-doing).

Debating Phrases

Chairing a Debate

- Will you please state your point in the form of a question.
- The speaker appears not to have understood your question. Will you please repeat / rephrase your question.
- Are there any further points?
- Will the speaker please make his concluding remarks.
- Debate time for / against has been exhausted.

The Merchant of Venice – Jozef Horemans

The Merchant of Venice is a Shakespeare play which exposes the follies of greed and self interest. In the story, Antonio secures a loan from the hated Jewish money lender, Shylock. The deal involves Antonio hubristically agreeing to forfeit a pound of his own flesh – in other words, his life, if he cannot repay the loan. In the picture, a vengeful and merciless Shylock demands his retribution. The ruling has to be upheld by the Venetian court, where the security and prosperity of the city depends on the rule of law being paramount. In the end, Shylock is thwarted by a legal technicality prohibiting him from shedding one drop of Antonio's blood.

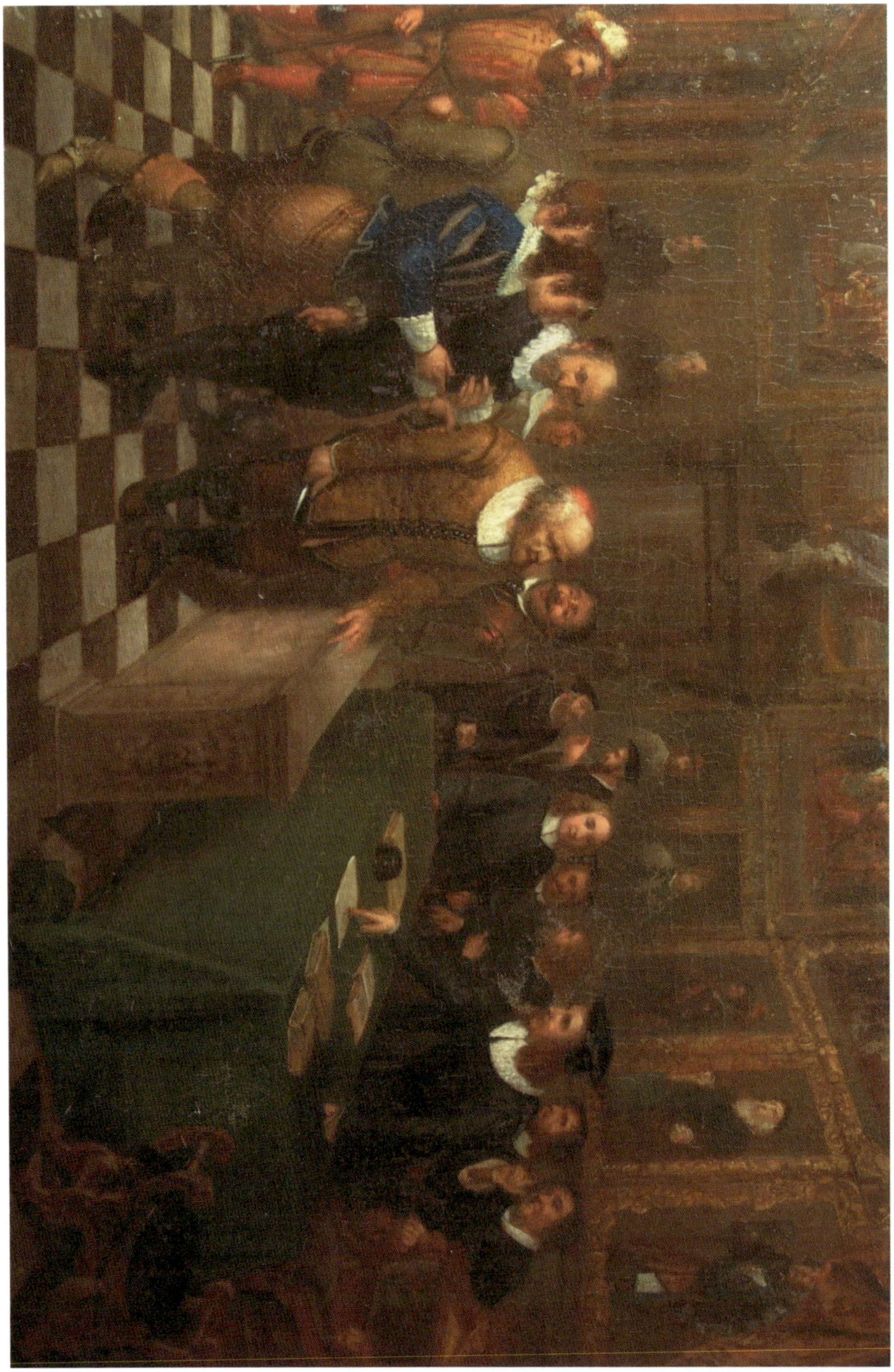

Yes, 'an eye for an eye' is a fair statement.

- One of the main purposes of the law is to provide fair retaliation for an offended party. This proverb defines and restricts the retaliation. The rule of law is fundamental to all civilizations. Without such basic laws there would be anarchy and no order in society. We need acceptable satisfaction when we have been wronged. We need real justice in our lives and in our societies.

- It's good to specify penalties for specific crimes, which are fitting in their severity. This prevents excessive punishment at the hands of either an avenging private party or the state. If someone stole some money, the victim might want to kill the man, which would be unfair. The rule stops people going too far in their punishments. Therefore it helps to create a fair and moral society.

- The concept encourages co-operation. If someone co-operates with you and works well together, you will work well with them and everyone is happy. If that person does not work well, or does something bad then you will do the same. Both sides know the rule, and under the rule they are better off if they work together. Therefore 'an eye for an eye' promotes peace, prosperity and good deeds in society and international relations. It's good for the economy because it encourages trust in your fellow man.

- A less well-established system for retribution of wrongs, feuds and vendettas, threatened the social fabric. The concept is one of common sense and reasonableness. It is important in understanding conflicts around the world, particularly in the context of Israel's foreign policy. Human society works best when people exchange one deed for another, be it good or bad – *Quid pro quo*.

- 'Let the punishment fit the crime' is a simple rule and if it was used more there would be less crime in society than there is today. This is also pretty fair when you think about it. It means that you know what your punishment will be so it's less cruel and dramatic. If you can't accept the punishment, don't do the crime. Simple.

- Not everybody shares the same values and if someone wants to go around hurting people he should know that there will be a punishment agreed on by the people in power. This helps people to learn proper values. The law creates equality between people and equality of values.

- 'Eye for an eye' is a good deterrent. During the Cold War, the United States knew they would be wiped out if they attacked Russia and Russia knew they would get the same if they attacked America. So neither power attacked each other and the Cold War ended peacefully without anyone being killed, without a shot even being fired. It's the only way to stop North Korea and Iran developing nuclear missiles.

No, 'an eye for an eye' is not a fair statement.

- 'An eye for an eye will make the whole world blind.' This was said by Gandhi and he meant that this attitude encourages a cycle of violence which only harms both sides. The rule is negative and aggressive. It explains some of the worst aspects of today's world; especially the war between Israel and Hamas – they are both just following what they believe is the word of God, but it causes killing and misery.

- Even though it may be hard to do in practice, certain belief systems (such as Christianity) teach individuals to forgive those who wrong them, rather than seek retribution for a wrong. This is much fairer and kinder. It's more logical and sensible not to let other people get you angry or waste your time with negative energy towards them. Better to forget about it and move on. Focus your energy in a positive way and forgive their stupidity.

- Other belief systems have better concepts, such as the Taoist wúwéi which encourages a wronged person to simply accept the crime and try to take the least aggressive action to correct it, if any action needs to be taken at all. The Asian system of avoiding conflict is better and more civilized. Eye for an eye is a western concept and is hateful. It punishes people but it doesn't help to educate criminals and improve the world.

- Buddhism has the concept of karma: you can take retribution, but that action will have consequences, the suffering will naturally return to the individual who was wronged (as well as the one who did the wrong-doing). This is a better way to consider punishments because it uses natural law and encourages people to settle their problems peacefully.

- 'Eye for an eye' is wrong because it could cause World War 3 and wipe out the human race. The idea is that if one country destroys a country with nuclear weapons, the other country will respond in the same and completely destroy the other country. This idea is MAD – Mutually Assured Destruction.

- The ethic of reciprocity: 'You should treat others as you would like to be treated.' Confucius, Epicurus, Buddha and Jesus all said this and it is one of the most important rules of civilization. These 4 men lived at a time in history when mankind was becoming more enlightened (about 2,000 years ago) and this forms the basis of the modern idea of human rights. Every human has the right to be treated fairly.

- The idea that 'two wrongs make a right' is a logical fallacy (A type of *tu quoque*). Tit for tat is negative and childish. The rule came about 3,000 years ago to serve a very primitive Bronze Age society but it is not relevant in the modern world. The rule comes from the Bible therefore it is the word of God but is that what we need today? A wrong is a wrong.

Game Theory

The following puzzle is found on dozens of websites.

The Prisoner's Dilemma

Two suspects are arrested by the police. The police have insufficient evidence for a conviction, and, having separated both prisoners, visit each of them to offer the same deal. If one testifies (defects) for the prosecution against the other and the other remains silent, the betrayer goes free and the silent accomplice receives the full 10-year sentence. If both remain silent, both prisoners are sentenced to only six months in jail for a minor charge. If each betrays the other, each receives a five-year sentence. Each prisoner must choose to betray the other or to remain silent. Each one is assured that the other would not know about the betrayal before the end of the investigation.

	Prisoner B Stays Silent	**Prisoner B Defects**
Prisoner A Stays Silent	Each serves 6 months	Prisoner A: 10 years Prisoner B: goes free
Prisoner A Defects	Prisoner A: goes free Prisoner B: 10 years	Each serves 5 years

How should the prisoners act?

The answer

In this game, as in all game theory, the only concern of each individual player (prisoner) is maximizing his/her own payoff, without any concern for the other player's payoff. The unique equilibrium is that rational choice leads the two players to both play *defect* even though each player's individual reward would be greater if they both played cooperatively.

In the classic form of this game, cooperating is strictly dominated by defecting, so that the only possible equilibrium for the game is for all players to defect. No matter what the other player does, one player will always gain a greater payoff by playing *defect*. Since in any situation playing *defect* is more beneficial than cooperating, all rational players will play *defect*, all things being equal.

In the **iterated prisoner's dilemma** the game is played repeatedly with players remembering previous actions of their opponent and changing their strategy accordingly. Thus each player has an opportunity to punish the other player for previous non-cooperative play. If the number of steps is known by both players in advance, economic theory says that the two players should defect again and again, no matter how many times the game is played. If the number of total games is not known or if the probability of the two players playing another game is sufficiently large, cooperation can be a stable strategy.

The best strategy in this type of game is the simplest, i.e. **tit for tat** with the player acting co-operatively in the first game after that, the player does what his opponent did on the previous move.

Vocab Refresh

Retaliate – hit back.

Reciprocate – reply in kind to what the other person does. If they give, you give.

Retribution – punishment / revenge. Just desserts.

Anarchy – a society or community with no authoritative order.

Avenge – the verb form of revenge.

Better off – wealthier, more satisfied, in an improved disposition than before.

Feud – violent, vicious or heated rivalry.

Vendetta – a private feud in which the members of the family of a murdered person seek to avenge the murder by killing the slayer or one of the slayer's relatives, esp. such vengeance as once practiced in Corsica and parts of Italy.

The social fabric – the strength of mutual values and bonds between members of a particular society.

Enlightened – broadly means wisdom or understanding enabling clarity of perception.

Tit for tat – repayment in kind, as for an injury; retaliation.

Primitive – basic and unsophisticated.

Mutually Assured Destruction – both attacker and defender are annihilated by nuclear weapons.

Deterrent – strength or ability to retaliate that creates enough fear of the consequences to stop (deter) others from attacking.

Quid pro quo – you scratch my back, I'll scratch yours. One thing in return for another, a favour for a favour, etc.

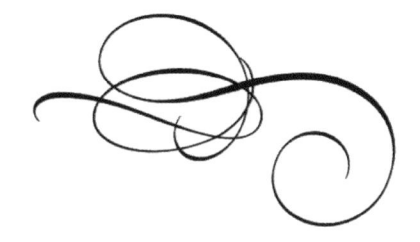

Debate 14 – Civil Liberties

Debate 14 – Civil Liberties

Should we be willing to give up our privacy for greater security from crime and terrorism?

Goals of the Lesson

- For students to become more familiar with the concepts and ethical basis of counter-terrorism.
- For students to practice debating, using persuasive devices and functional phrases.
- For students to find some form of consensus on the issue.

Rhetoric

Discuss and demonstrate these figures of speech with the class and explain that people who are able to speak forcefully and persuasively often use devices like this. Tell the students that you would like them to try and use these devices during the debate.

1. **Epanorthosis** – immediate and emphatic self-correction, often following a slip of the tongue.

'The psychologist known as Sigmund Fraud – *Freud*, I mean!'

'Man has parted company with his trusty friend the horse and has sailed into the azure with the eagles, eagles being represented by the infernal combustion engine – er er, *internal* combustion engine. [loud laughter] Internal combustion engine! Engine!' ~ Winston Churchill

2. **Euphemism** – substitution of a less offensive or more agreeable term for another.

'Ethnic cleansing' for mass slaughter of civilians / genocide.

3. **Epistrophe** – the repetition of the same word or group of words at the end of successive clauses. The counterpart of **anaphora**. Also known as **antistrophe**.

'...government of the people, by the people, for the people, shall not perish from the earth.'~ Abraham Lincoln

The 'Yes we can' tagline used by Barack Obama in his 2008 Election campaign speeches.

Logical Fallacies

The Logical Fallacy is a rhetorical device which has no grounding in actual fact and is used by people to unfairly gain the upper hand in debates. Being able to spot such a flaw goes a long way to invalidating an opponent's argument.

1. **Fallacy of the General Rule** – assuming that something true in general is true in every possible case. Similarly, there are times when certain laws should be broken. For example, ambulances are allowed to break speed laws.

The much coveted principle of free speech is not as untouchable as many like to believe. Limitations include hate crimes, shouting fire in a crowded theatre, incitement to violence and defamation.

2. **False Cause** – *post hoc ergo propter hoc*. Sequence and correlation do not mean causation.

As ice cream sales increase, the rate of drowning deaths increases sharply. Therefore, ice cream consumption causes drowning.

Cargo cults are a good example of false causation. In many Pacific Island communities, people superstitiously believed that the manufactured goods Westerners brought and arrived in were intended for them as messages from their ancestors. As a result, the islanders set up elaborate rituals to summon the cargo to return.

3. **False Compromise** – the mistaken belief, usually arising out of ignorance, that it is best to give both sides of the argument equal credence or emphasis, even though one side is actually wrong. Misguided fairness. Also called **argument to moderation** or *argumentum ad temperantiam*.

An example is 'balanced' coverage in the media even when one of the positions being argued is a ludicrous view of a tiny minority. For entertainment purposes and for ethical reasons of trying to and appear unbiased, this may be fine but logically it is irrelevant.

Preamble

Adapted from Wikipedia.

Civil liberties are freedoms that protect the individual from the government. Civil liberties set limits for government so that it cannot abuse its power and interfere with the lives of its citizens. These include:

- Freedom of religion
- Freedom from religion
- Freedom of speech
- The right to a fair trial
- The right to own property
- The right to privacy

The formal concept of civil liberties dates back to the Magna Carta of 1215 which in turn was based on pre-existing documents. Democratic Republics such as the United States have a constitution, a bill of rights and similar constitutional documents that enumerate and seek to guarantee civil liberties.

The bone of contention which this debate centers around is that periodically, in states of war and emergency, governments have often suspended or completely withdrawn elements of civil liberty in the name of national security.

An interesting aspect to the debate occurred in June 2008 when British politician and Shadow Home Secretary David Davies resigned over what he described as the 'erosion of civil liberties' in reference to new anti-terrorism laws allowing terror suspects to be detained without trial for up to 42 days (previously 28 days). Davies perceived this to be an infringement to Habeas Corpus established in the Magna Carta in 1215. Habeas Corpus is an enshrined right in British and American law which can stop a trail taking place if the defendant is not there in person. The legislation in question was subsequently defeated in the House of Lords (which delays it for up to 12 months). In addition to this, in 2012 The UK government proposed new powers for total internet surveillance which were opposed by many as unnecessary and a dangerous infringement of ordinary Britons' civil liberties.

Counter Terrorism refers to the practices that governments, militaries, police departments and corporations adopt in response to terrorist threats and/or acts, both real and imputed. Unlike anti-terrorism which is mainly defensive, counter-terrorism includes offensive strategies intended to prevent a belligerent, in a broader conflict, from successfully using the tactic of terrorism. The U.S. military definition, compatible with the definitions used by NATO and many other militaries, is 'Operations that include the offensive measures taken to prevent, deter, pre-empt, and respond to terrorism.' In other words, counter-terrorism is a set of techniques for denying an opponent the use terrorism-based tactics.

What exactly does counter-terrorism in the United States encompass?

- Guantanamo Bay
- Torturing suspects – water boarding
- US Patriot Act
- Snooping on phone calls
- Snooping on emails
- Monitoring internet activity
- Secret record searches
- Detention and deportation of non-citizens
- Monitoring of religious institutions
- Airport screening
- Searches on the basis of ethnicity

The US Patriot Act is a controversial law giving the government in America broad powers to search telephone, e-mail communications, medical, financial and other records and regulate financial transactions. It also eases the ability to detain and deport immigrants suspected of terrorism-related acts. It was signed into law by George W Bush in October 2001. Despite being passed with large majorities, several legal challenges have been brought against the act and Federal courts have ruled that a number of provisions are unconstitutional.

―

The big issue in this argument is whether it is fair to snoop on innocent people's emails and phone calls, internet surfing history, etc. This debate is not limited the context of the United States. The ongoing Israeli-Palestinian conflict, Syrian Civil War, and Colombian Civil War or indeed American and other invasions of countries around the world are all examples of conflicts where terrorism is present and counter-terrorism measures are used. Therefore it is more viable to make this a hypothetical argument concerning how far can governments go in eliminating threats in the world at large.

Debating Phrases

Chairing – Closing the Debate

- The debate is now closed. We will move into voting procedures.
- The motion will now be put to the vote.
- Will all those in favour of the resolution please raise their hands.
- Will all those opposed to / against the resolution, please raise their hands.
- Are there any abstentions?
- Will all those abstaining, please raise their hands.

Themis – Legislative Council Building of Hong Kong (built 1912)

Themis or Lady Justice, is a common figure in European mythology. She stands blindfolded and holding a pair of scales, representing impartiality and the fairness of the law. In the left hand she wields power with the Sword of Justice, representing the state's monopoly on the legitimate use of coercive force. This statue is similar to the famous gold figure standing atop the Old Bailey in London. The location of the building (formerly the Supreme Court) is a center for protests today.

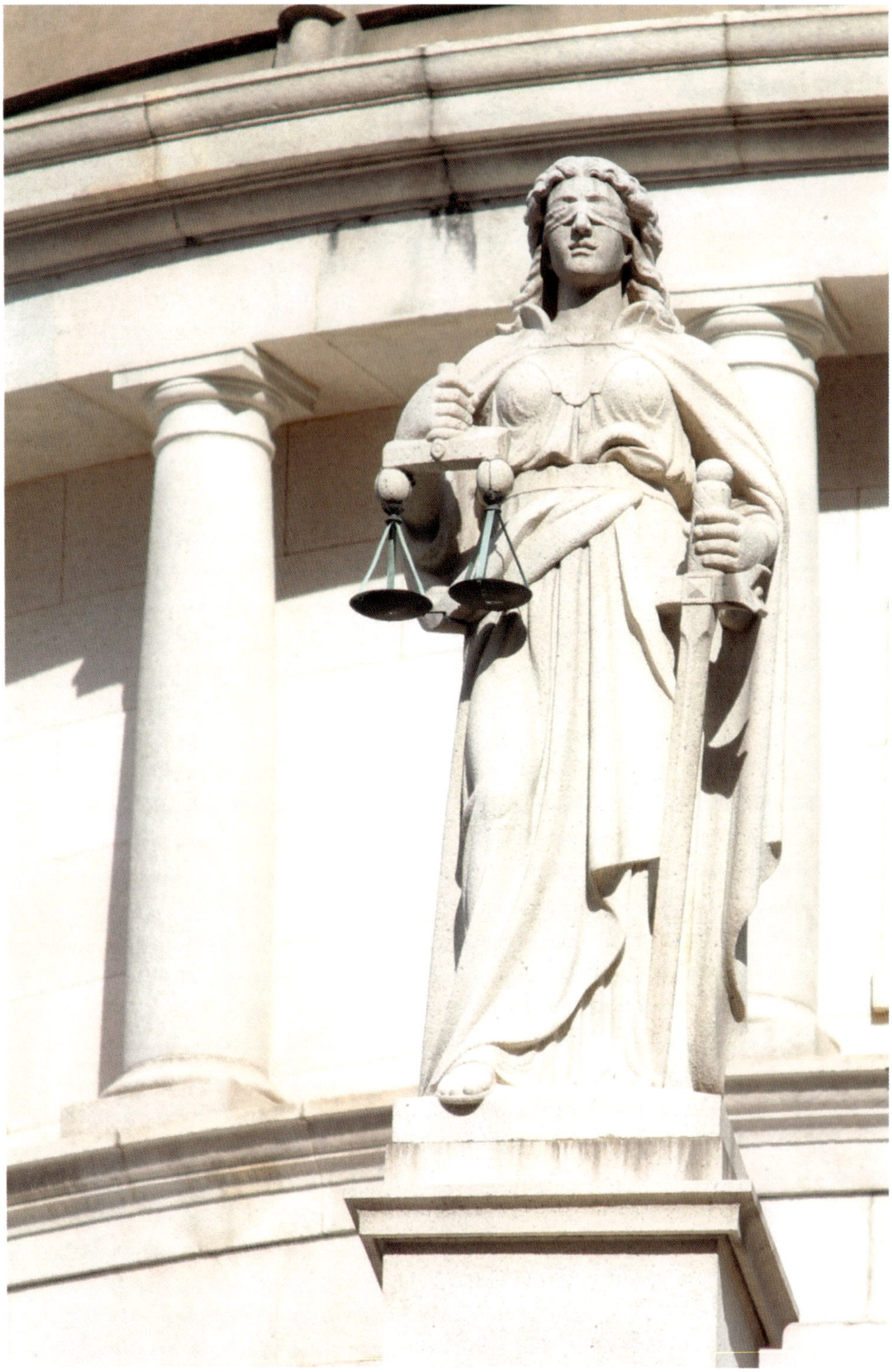

Yes, security is more important than civil liberties.

- Threats need to be pre-empted. Pre-emptive action is a legitimate strategy. Good intelligence is necessary to win wars so recording phone conversations and reading emails is fine. The government is right not to take risks. Abraham Lincoln is praised for suspending civil liberties during the Civil War. People should understand the need to sacrifice some freedom during war and right now the developed world is at war. It's the War on Terror.

- Governments have to invade other countries to stop terrorists hiding or being supported. Some governments cannot control their people, so other countries must do it to protect themselves. If innocent people are killed by the US military, that's because their governments have not done enough to stop the terrorists. We live in a time when our enemies live among us. The rules have to change to fight this threat.

- Surveillance reduces crime and helps people catch the bad guys. Terrorism has gone down recently and we should be thankful. Terrorists are plotting all over the world to kill innocent people and they must be stopped. Anyone with common sense knows that when a country is in danger, civil liberties are a luxury. In fact in most countries in the world people have few civil liberties and they don't complain. People should remember what it was like during World War 2 when we were fighting fascism….

- The government are not going to read normal people's email and listen to ordinary phone calls. Why would they? It's so full of boring, meaningless information and there's so much of it that they don't have the manpower to read it all even if they wanted to. They are only interested in the people who have been recognized as threats. This is how plots get stopped. We should be glad more people have not died.

- If you're against snooping on emails and phone calls, you are as bad as the terrorists. You are either with us or against us. Beating terrorists involves all parts of society and many government agencies. Counter-terrorism needs an increase in police and intelligence work. This means secretly recording telephone and internet communications. This is necessary and people should be happy we have the technology to beat them.

- Terrorists communicate over the internet. The government have the power to monitor this and they should. It saves people's lives. People who have done nothing wrong have nothing to worry about. The government should be respected by everyone because they are trying to protect us. Spying is a necessary evil. Every country does it and we need to be the best at it.

No, security is not more important than civil liberties.

- The problem with secret snooping is that it gets the wrong people. The police often have a 'shoot to kill policy' with suspected terrorists which means they sometimes kill the wrong people. In London in 2005 the police mistook Jean Charles de Menezes for a terrorist and shot him eight times when he was getting on the subway. Since when did police have the right to kill unarmed civilians?

- Detention without trail is a violation of basic human rights, plus it runs the risk of torture. Human rights do not stop at borders. If we give the military the power to arrest anybody, the results could be dangerous. It could make the terrorist threat worse rather than stop it. The police and military should not be able to do whatever they want, wherever they want. We have LAWS which are supposed to stop this.

- Invasion of privacy is unfair (tapping telephones, random searches, hidden cameras etc.). Mass Surveillance of a whole population is totalitarian like George Orwell's 1984. Intelligence and screening is often directed at ethnic or religious groups. In airports a person could be stopped, searched and ashamed just because he or she looks like an Arab. We need to fight terrorism but human rights must also be considered.

- Surveillance of a whole populations internet on the basis of anti-terrorism is silly, costly and not worth it. If the government does this then everyone becomes a suspect. Everyone's bank transactions can be seen. The government will then begin to control even more of our private lives. Then we will become a fascist state where everyone lives in fear. Benjamin Franklin said: 'Those who would give up essential liberty to purchase a little temporary safety deserve neither liberty nor safety.'

- Sometimes the army beat, torture, drug prisoners so they admit to something or so they can get information, targets, names, etc. This is against the Geneva Convention but some countries don't care about that. Someone needs to make sure they obey these basic rules otherwise we will live in a police state. Funny how the people are not allowed to read the government's emails. Politicians do far more dirty dealing than citizens. What hypocrites.

- What people do in the privacy of their own homes is up to them. It is not the business of the government or the police. I don't want a TV camera watching what I do in my own home. Nobody wants that. Why should people be reading my emails and Facebook chats? Why should people be looking at my internet history? It is supposed to private information. If the government wants to see it then they should have a good reason and apply for a court order from a judge.

- The terrorist threat is actually small but the government likes to spread fear so they can control us easily. People are way too paranoid about terrorism. Really. Do you know how many people die in car accidents alone every year? Let's just say it's many times the number of people who died once on 9/11. We are obsessed with fear. If we care that much, why don't we put roll cages in all cars? Why don't we eat healthier?

Internet Freedom

Ask the students to write a letter to Amnesty International or Avaaz complaining about increasing internet censorship in their country and how it is a dangerous and unnecessary infringement of human rights.

Vocab Refresh

Pre-emptive action – striking someone before they strike you, or at least taking measures in preparation of a conflict.

Legitimate strategy – a legal and fair way to deal with a problem.

Sacrifice – to give up something for the greater good, or for future gain.

Manpower – the amount of human resources available to complete a project.

Snooping on emails and phone calls – spying on people.

Government agencies – government departments, with appointed chiefs.

Counter-terrorism – offensive measure used to deal with threats.

Surveillance – watching / monitoring without people's consent.

Detention without trail – imprisoning someone with giving the access to legal rights.

A violation of basic human rights – a breach of human rights.

Totalitarian like George Orwell's 1984 – Complete control by the government over the lives of its citizens.

Fascism – a system often led by a dictator where the upper classes suppress the lower classes and emphasize aggressive nationalism and racism.

Geneva Convention – An international legal code and treaty signed by every nation concerning the rules for conduct of war.

Hypocrite – a sanctimonious person who says one thing but does not follow it himself.

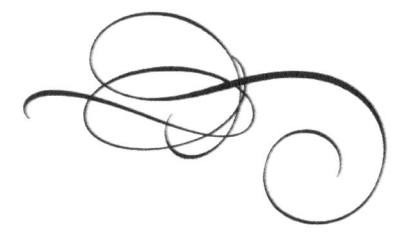

Debate 15 – Capital Punishment

Debate 15 – Capital Punishment

Should the death penalty be an option for the most serious crimes?

Goals of the Lesson

- For students to become more familiar with the arguments surrounding capital punishment
- For students to practice debating, using persuasive devices and functional phrases
- For students to find some form of consensus on the issue

Rhetoric

Discuss and demonstrate these figures of speech with the class and explain that people who are able to speak forcefully and persuasively often use devices like this. Tell the students that you would like them to try and use these devices during the debate.

1. **Euphony** – the opposite of **cacophony**. I.e. pleasant sounding.

'Season of mists and mellow fruitfulness,
Close bosom-friend of the maturing sun;
Conspiring with him how to load and bless
With fruit the vines that round the thatch-eves run'
~ Keats, *To Autumn*

2. **Hendiadys** – a form of **periphrasis / circumlocution**; using two nouns when the normal structure would be a noun and a modifier. The splitting of two adjectives, verbs and other word pairs can also fall under hendiadys.

'Life's but a walking shadow, a poor player
That struts and frets his hour upon the stage
And then is heard no more: it is a tale
Told by an idiot, full of sound and fury,
Signifying nothing.'
~ Shakespeare, *The Tragedy of Macbeth*

The more common forms would be the simpler 'frettingly struts' and 'furious sound'.

3. **Hendiatris** – use of three nouns to express one idea. Three is very much a magic number in rhetoric.

'Wine, women and song.'

Logical Fallacies

The Logical Fallacy is a rhetorical device which has no grounding in actual fact and is used by people to unfairly gain the upper hand in debates. Being able to spot such a flaw goes a long way to invalidating an opponent's argument.

1. **Genetic Fallacy** – tainting the argument by looking at the irrelevant background of the arguer or argument rather than the argument itself. Similar to **ad hominem** and **poisoning the wells**.

'I wouldn't believe anything you read in the 'liberal media'.'

2. **Having Your Cake** – **failure to assert**, or **diminished claim** – almost claiming something, but backing out. Can lead to **equivocation**.

'It may be, as some suppose, that ghosts can only be seen by certain so-called sensitives, who are possibly special mutations with, perhaps, abnormally extended ranges of vision and hearing. Yet some claim we are all sensitives.' ~ Don Lindsay, *A List of Fallacious Arguments*

3. **Hypothesis Contrary to Fact** – arguing as if something had already happened when in fact it hadn't.

'If Hitler had not invaded Russia and opened up two military fronts, the Nazis would surely have won the war.'

Preamble

From Wikipedia.

Execution of criminals and political opponents has been used by nearly all societies – both to punish crime and to suppress political dissent. In most places that practice capital punishment it is reserved for murder, espionage, treason, or as part of military justice. In some countries sexual crimes such as rape, adultery, incest and sodomy carry the death penalty as do religious crimes such as apostasy (the formal renunciation of the state religion). In many countries that use the death penalty drug trafficking is also a capital offence. In China, human trafficking and serious cases of corruption are punished by the death penalty. In militaries around the world courts-martial have imposed death sentences for offences such as cowardice, desertion, insubordination, and mutiny.

Severe historical penalties include the breaking wheel, boiling to death, flaying, slow slicing, disembowelment, crucifixion, impalement, crushing (including crushing by elephant), stoning, and execution by burning, dismemberment, sawing, or decapitation.

In 1700s Britain there were 222 crimes which were punishable by death, including crimes such as cutting down a tree or stealing an animal. Thanks to the notorious Bloody Code, 18th century (and early 19th century) Britain was a hazardous place to live. For example, Michael Hammond and his sister, Ann, whose ages were given as 7 and 11, were reportedly hanged at King's Lynn on Wednesday, September 28, 1708 for theft. The local press did not, however, consider the executions of two children newsworthy.

Although many are executed in China each year in modern times, there was a time in Tang Dynasty China when the death penalty was abolished. This was in the year 747, enacted by Emperor Taizong (712–756) who was the only person in China with the authority to sentence criminals to execution. Even then capital punishment was relatively infrequent with only 24 executions in the year 730 and 58 executions in the year 736. Two hundred years later there was a form of execution called Ling Chi (slow slicing), or death by a thousand cuts, used in China from roughly 900 to its abolition in 1905.

The 12th century Sephardic legal scholar, Moses Maimonides, wrote 'It is better and more satisfactory to acquit a thousand guilty persons than to put a single innocent man to death.' He argued that executing an accused criminal on anything less than absolute certainty would lead to a slippery slope of decreasing burdens of proof, until we would be convicting merely "according to the judge's caprice." His concern was maintaining popular respect for law, and he saw errors of commission as much more threatening than errors of omission.

Among countries around the world, almost all European and many Pacific Area states (including Australia and New Zealand) and Canada have abolished capital punishment. In Latin America most states have completely abolished the use of capital punishment while some countries such as Brazil allow for capital punishment only in exceptional situations, such as treason committed during wartime. The United States (the federal government and 36 of the states), Guatemala, most of the Caribbean and the majority of democracies in Asia (e.g. Japan and India) and Africa (e.g. Botswana and Zambia) retain it. South Africa, which is probably the most developed African nation and which has been a democracy since 1994, does not have the death penalty. This fact is currently quite controversial in that country due to the high levels of violent crime including murder and rape.

Trends in most of the world have long been to move to less painful or more humane executions. France developed the guillotine for this reason in the final years of the 18th century while Britain banned drawing and quartering in the early 19th century. Hanging by turning the victim off a ladder or by dangling them from the back of a moving cart, which causes death by suffocation, was replaced by hanging where the subject is dropped a longer distance to dislocate the neck and sever the spinal cord. In the U.S., the electric chair and the gas chamber were introduced as more humane alternatives to hanging but have been almost entirely superseded by lethal injection which in turn has been criticized as being too painful. Nevertheless, some countries still employ slow hanging methods, beheading by sword and even stoning although the latter is rarely employed.

Since World War II there has been a consistent trend towards abolishing the death penalty. In 1977, 16 countries were abolitionist. By 2008, 93 countries had abolished capital punishment, 9 had done so for all offences except under special circumstances and 35 had not used it for at least 10 years or under a moratorium. Sixty actively retained the death penalty.

Iran, despite its ratification of the Convention on the Rights of the Child and International Covenant on Civil and Political Rights, is currently the world's biggest executioner of child offenders, for which it has received international condemnation; the country's record is the focus of the Stop Child Executions Campaign. Iran accounts for two-thirds of the global total of such executions, and currently has roughly 140 people on death row for crimes committed as juveniles (up from 71 in 2007).

Debating Phrases

Challenges

- That's absurd.
- That's pretty small beer.
- It's self-evidently nonsense.
- You are damaging your credibility.
- This is the rebuttal to the Conservatives.
- They don't like it, Mr Speaker.
- Isn't it true you…?

Hanging Witches (1650)

This image is found in Ralph Gardiner's *England's Grievance Discovered in Relation to the Coal Trade*, 1655. The witches in question were imprisoned and executed in Newcastle upon Tyne after a Scottish trickster (pictured on the right) convinced the city leaders that witchcraft was rife in the town and that for twenty shillings a piece, he could expose them. The witch finder was later arrested and hanged. He admitted causing the death of two-hundred and twenty women in England and Scotland.

In his book, addressed to Oliver Cromwell, Gardiner exposes the cruel and foolish city authorities for a variety of poor policies and unfair governance. Gardiner called the rule of the Magistrates of Newcastle "unchristian, illegal, oppressive and repugnant to the Laws of England."

Great Debates

Yes, capital punishment should be an option.

- An eye for an eye, tooth for a tooth, therefore death for death is appropriate. If someone killed my family I would kill them, without question. Any parent would do the same. The murder victim's families want to see justice. They have a right to justice and that means the death sentence. We want real punishments.

- The methods of killing are now humane. Lethal injection means that the prisoner feels very little before he dies. The old way of executing people was cruel but now it is just like pressing a button and no-one gets hurt. This means that it is much cheaper to execute people rather than keep them in prison for the whole of their lives.

- We need more public executions of high ranking government officials who are caught committing war crimes. Imagine what it would do for our image if we got rid of a few of those rats. Saddam Hussein and Gaddafi were a cruel barbaric dictators and they deserved the death penalty.

^ Iconoclast421 – anythingexceptthetruth.blogspot.com

- The death penalty is a good deterrent. People think twice about committing a murder if they know they will be executed for it. It also prevents people committing crimes again, because they are already dead. Dead people cannot be a danger to society.

- People say two wrongs don't make a right but I believe you must fight fire with fire. The death penalty is morally right, not wrong. Death penalty supporters say that society has the moral right – and duty – to take the lives of those who kill others. A person who has killed another is unfit to live in a human society.

- Money is not an unlimited resource. Killing criminals saves millions of dollars that would have to be spent on prisons, etc. The money that we save can be spent on looking after the sick, the old and the young, rather than murderers and rapists.

- Capital punishment permanently removes the worst criminals from society and means the world is safer for the rest of us. Singapore is one of the safest places in the world and they execute more people per capita than any other country. Tough laws work. Plus, DNA testing and other methods of modern crime scene science can now effectively eliminate almost all uncertainty as to a person's guilt or innocence.

- Life in prison does not work. It does not change the criminals mind and criminals see prison as a holiday camp. In European countries prisoners can surf the internet and go on day-trips. Murders often 'get off' after about 8 years by claiming mental illness or appealing.

No, capital punishment should never be an option.

- Wrongful executions. Many innocent people have been executed throughout history. DNA evidence has proved that many people did not commit the crimes they were killed for. Someone once said that 'It is better to let 1000 guilty people go free than execute one innocent man.'

- 'Distrust all in whom the urge to punish is powerful'. This was said by Nietzsche. George W Bush executed more people than any previous governor of Texas. Do you trust him? Two wrongs don't make a right.

- A lifetime in jail is worse than execution. If I had to spend all my life locked in a room with no freedom I would probably prefer to die. Killing them is the easy way out. We should make criminals suffer!

- Christian teachings say forgive people. Buddhism also disagrees with violence and the death penalty. The Bible says 'Thou shall not kill.' If someone does something bad to you and they are sorry, you should forgive them. What is wrong with this idea?

- Killing people for whatever reason is cruel and barbaric. It is what people did thousands of years ago before they learned to be civilized human beings. We live in a modern world now, so there is no reason to kill anyone during peacetime. The death penalty is a primitive way of dealing with people.

- There is no philosophical (thoughtful) justification for revenge. Revenge is just a dark, twisted desire to inflict damage on another person so that you'll feel better. The great thing you can do to heal humanity's karma is to accept abuse without holding a grudge or inflicting damage back and continuing the cycle. Every attack is a call for help.

- The death penalty is a bad deterrent. It doesn't deter people from committing really serious crimes, certainly no more than life imprisonment. Most murders are done in the 'heat of passion' when a person cannot think rationally. How can a person even have time to think of fear in the heat of passion?

- The death penalty encourages a 'culture of violence' because the population become brutalized towards violence and killings. This will mean more murders, more strife, more violence and crime. The death penalty could have the opposite effected to its intended one.

Condemned to Death

Discuss the historical figure of Socrates with the class. Explain that despite being a decorated war hero and esteemed teacher in the city of Athens, he was a political nuisance and caused a lot of trouble by questioning the government and making them look stupid. Socrates reasoned that he was clever because he knew that he knew nothing, whereas the city leaders assumed they knew everything. This enraged the Athenian lawmakers to such a degree that they tried him and sentences him to death – a sentence which he accepted. Give each student a copy of the following (abridged) text and practice reading it aloud.

On Being Condemned to Death – Socrates (469–399 B.C.)

Athenians, you will criticize those who wish to insult the government by putting that wise man, Socrates, to death. Because those who insult you and criticize your government believe that I am wise, though I am not. If you had waited for a short time, this would have happened anyway. Look at my age; it is far advanced in life, and near death.

But I say this not to you all, but to those only who have condemned me to die. Perhaps you think, O Athenians, that I have been convicted through the weak arguments of my defence, by which I might have persuaded you, had I thought it right to do and say anything so that I might escape punishment. But the truth is quite the opposite: I have been convicted through weakness indeed, but not of arguments, but of daring and nerve, and of the feeling to say the things to you that you wanted to hear. Things that are unworthy of me, like the things you are used to hearing from others.

I did not think it would be right for me to do anything unworthy of a freeman just to avoid danger. Nor do I regret not defending myself, but I would much rather choose to die, than live in that way. Neither in a trial nor in battle is it right that I or anyone else should do everything he can to avoid death; for in battle a man might escape death by surrendering and throwing himself at the mercy of his enemy. And there are many other ways in every danger, to avoid death, if a man dares to do and say everything.

But this is not difficult, O Athenians, to escape death, but it is much more difficult to avoid wickedness, for it runs swifter than death. And now I, being slow and aged, am overtaken by the slower of the two; but my accusers, being strong and active, have been overtaken by the swifter, wickedness. And now I leave, condemned by you to death; but they are condemned by truth, as guilty of evil and injustice: and I abide my sentence and so do they. So be it, and I think that it is for the best.

Vocab Refresh

Humane – characterized by tenderness, compassion, and sympathy for people and animals, esp. for the suffering or distressed: *humane treatment of horses*.

Lethal injection – execution by deadly poison injected into the condemned man. Apparently this hurts a lot…

Barbaric – without civilizing influences; uncivilized; primitive: *barbaric invaders*.

High ranking government officials – powerful party bosses.

DNA evidence – Deoxyribonucleic Acid, viz. evidence derived from.

The urge to punish – i.e. someone who wants to punish.

Primitive – basic, caveman-like.

Deterrent – something that deters.

Think rationally – to think using logic and reason, like any sane person.

Brutalized – having become cruel and barbaric.

Twisted – sick, perverse, abnormal and negative mental behaviour.

Inflict – to hand out or impose something bad on another person, causing suffering.

Karma – a Buddhist belief that if you do bad things, bad thing will happen to you.

Strife – difficulty, hardship and woe.

Passion – a feeling or quality of immense love, energy and enthusiasm.

Deterrent – a factor that puts people off doing something, like a warning.

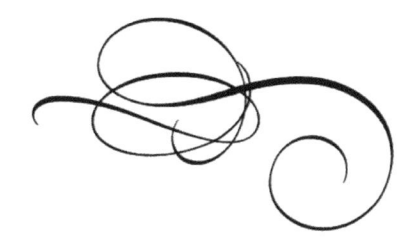

Debate 16 – Crime & Punishment

Debate 16 – Crime & Punishment

Should punishment be more important than rehabilitation in criminal justice?

Goals of the Lesson

- For students to become more familiar with the issues concerning crime and punishment.
- For students to practice debating, using persuasive devices and functional phrases.
- For students to find some form of consensus on the issue.

Rhetoric

Discuss and demonstrate these figures of speech with the class and explain that people who are able to speak forcefully and persuasively often use devices like this. Tell the students that you would like them to try and use these devices during the debate.

1. **Kenning** – a figure of speech used in Old English and Old Norse literature where a single-word noun is replaced with a compound word giving it a more evocative feel. A type of **circumlocution** and **metonymy**.

'Sky-candle' for *sun*. ~ *Exodus*, 10th Century poem.
'Whale-way' for *sea*. ~ *The Seafarer*, 8th Century poem.
'Battle-sweat' for *blood*. ~ *Beowulf*
'Feeder of ravens' for *warrior*. ~ *Glymdrápa*, 9th Century Norwegian poem.

2. **Pleonasm** – a repetition or use of extra unneeded words. Often considered bad style or grammar but can be used to give an extra bit of meaning or feeling. It is a feature many English idiom phrases. See **tautology**.

'This was the most unkindest cut of all.' ~ Shakespeare, *The Tragedy of Julius Caesar*

'Let me tell you this, when social workers offer you, *free, gratis and for nothing*, something to hinder you from swooning, which with them is an obsession, it is useless to recoil …' ~ Samuel Beckett, *Molloy*

Hypallage – changing the word order so that the adjective modifies an unusual noun.

'Restless night' – The night was not restless, but the person who was awake through it was.

'Fitting the clumsy helmets just in time' ~ Wilfred Owen, *Dulce et Decorum est*

Logical Fallacies

The Logical Fallacy is a rhetorical device which has no grounding in actual fact and is used by people to unfairly gain the upper hand in debates. Being able to spot such a flaw goes a long way to invalidating an opponent's argument.

1. **Inconsistency**.

'The declining life expectancy in the former Soviet Union is due to the failures of communism. But, the quite high infant mortality rate in the United States is not a failure of capitalism.' ~ Carl Sagan, *The Fine Art of Baloney Detection*

2. **Inflation of Conflict** – exploiting a small disagreement in order to validate a much larger argument.

Two historians debated whether Hitler killed five million Jews or six million Jews. A Holocaust denier argued that this disagreement made *his* claim credible, even though his death count is three to ten times smaller than the known minimum. ~ Don Lindsay, *A List of Fallacious Arguments*

Arguing that because some parts of some of Shakespeare plays were probably written by someone else, then Shakespeare did not exist at all.

3. **Internal Contradiction** – saying two contradictory things in the same argument.

The Qur'an attacks those who worship anyone besides God (e.g. angels or prophets) because those can neither create, nor give life, nor cause anyone to die. Yet, the Qur'an explicitly states that one angel or several angels causes certain people to die. ~ answering-islam.org/Quran/Contra

Great Debates

Preamble

From Wikipedia.

Society expects the criminal justice system to **punish** and **rehabilitate** criminals. Punishment and rehabilitation are two of the four objectives of the system, the other two being **deterrence** and **incapacitation**. Many people throughout history have argued about which is more effective, punishment or rehabilitation. In the United States, punishment has always been the primary goal when dealing with criminals. The effectiveness of punishment and rehabilitation has to be analyzed to see:

1. the effects on offenders
2. the effects on victims
3. the effect on society
4. the fiscal impact

The Classical School of Criminology argues that punishment creates deterrence and the Positive School of Criminology argues that rehabilitation reduces recidivism.

Forms of punishment include:
- Incarceration
- Corporal punishment (public beatings)
- Capital punishment (execution)
- Hard labour

Forms of rehabilitation include:
- Drug therapy for addicts
- Psychological counseling for people from abusive households
- Education and training
- Community service / supervision
- Probation

Rehabilitation is based on creating a change in the criminal's attitude or resources so that crime is neither a desired nor necessary activity. Punishment is geared toward repentance and sorrow through physical and mental hardship.

The majority of society, including victims of crime, prefer swift punishment to rehabilitation through community supervision. According to the American Bureau of Justice Sourcebook of

Statistics, more than three-quarters of the public see punishment as the primary justification for sentencing. They also report that more than 70 percent believe that incapacitation is the only sure way to prevent future crimes, and more than three-quarters believe that the courts are too easy on criminals. Public opinion supports the increased use of prisons to give criminals just desserts. When a victim or the victim's family feels that their offender does not receive the appropriate sentence, it causes emotional stress.

Incarceration has many effects on the offender's psychological well-being. When an offender is separated from his family, it causes severe depression. Supporters of rehabilitation versus punishment argue that sentencing offenders to incarceration hurt the family structure by contributing to single parenting. They also argue that punishment causes social disorientation, alienation, and also increases the risk of recidivism. When an offender is released from incarceration, they face social isolation, stigmatism, economic and employment challenges. Rehabilitation through community supervision eliminates many of these issues, such as the economic and employment factor. Probation allows offenders to remain with their families, continue working or find employment under close supervision.

Research also shows that repeat crime following release from prison is as high as 63 percent and most prison inmates had arrest records and convictions prior to their current offence.

Debating Phrases

<u>Challenges</u> – From Prime Minister's Questions between Gordon Brown and David Cameron

- What's your definition of …?
- If you do not recognize that then you cannot begin to recognize the answers.
- Do you agree with me that …?
- Can anyone here say, that they don't …?
- Doesn't he understand that …?

The Panopticon Blueprint – Jeremy Bentham (1791)

The Panopticon was an Enlightenment design for the most suitable prison possible. The concept could be used in all sorts of authoritarian adaptions from hospitals to schools to offices, allowing all to be watched from a single point in the center of the building.

Previously, in a newly industrialized Britain with its bloated criminal population, prisons had been foul places where disease and death were commonplace. Bentham believed he could reinvigorate prisons, society and industry through this architectural design. The Panopticon was seen as a more humane, healthy and efficient housing for such a public burden.

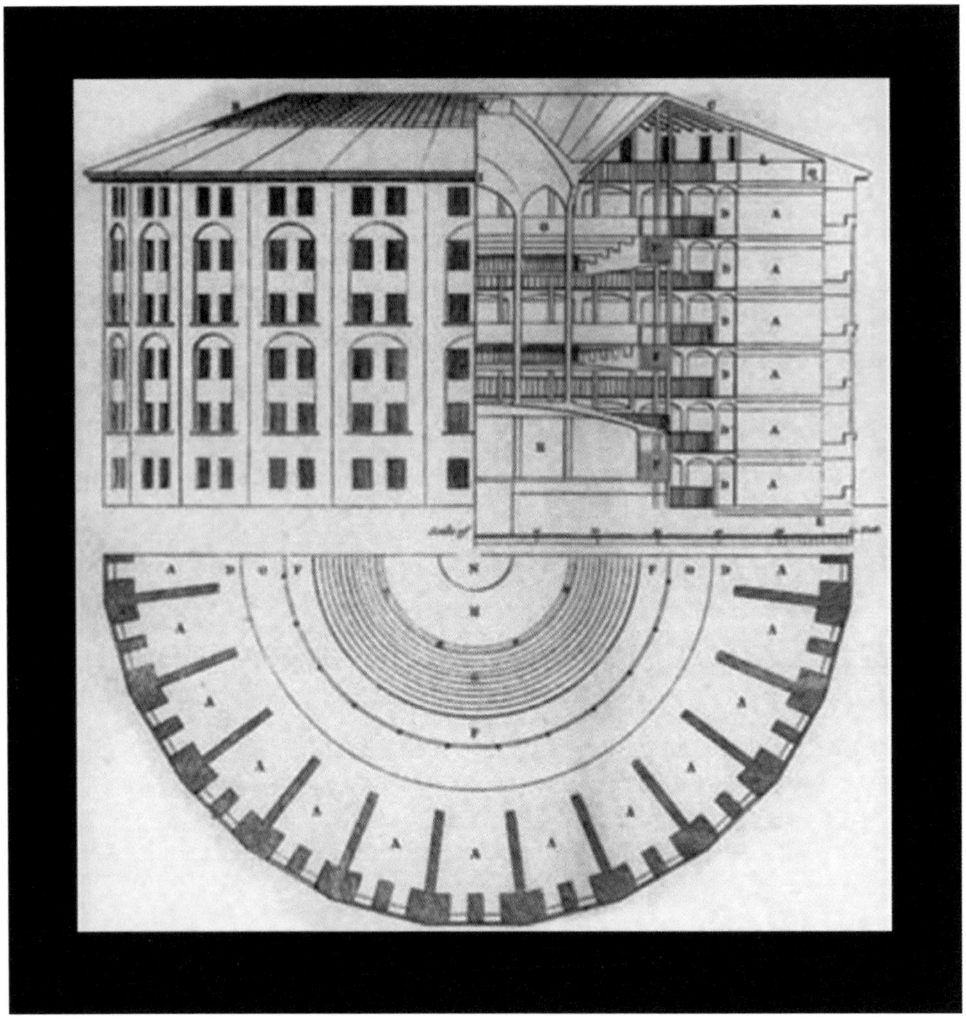

Yes, criminals should be punished.

- The fear of punishment is a good deterrent – it clearly works. Sometimes punishment in the form of violence and hardship are the only things that people understand. Most criminals are too stupid to realize that they have done something wrong, therefore rehab is wasted on them.

- Criminals deserve punishment. They have committed a crime and they cannot take it back. They cannot turn back the clock so they have to be dealt with in a way that equals their crime. Anything less is an insult to the victims. We all want to see justice.

- Punishment means they are less likely to re-offend. Punishment hurts people and no-one likes to be hurt again. Fear is how you train animals like horses and dogs. It is an effective way to teach people the difference between right and wrong if they refuse to learn it the sensible way. Prison should be about punishment as a last resort for people in society who do wrong. It gets results.

- Rehab programs cost money. Taxpayers' money can be better spent on more worthy and effective remedies. The money spent on soft solutions it is often wasted. The criminals don't always respond to rehab. Let the money for rehab be spent on people who are already genuinely sorry for what they have done.

- Why are we being such a soft society? This will lead to our ruin. What message do soft solutions send to criminals and potential criminals? It says, we will let you off and give you money and pampering.

- Letting criminals out early is dangerous. It's irresponsible and bad for society. It means that good people who pay their taxes do not feel safe to walk the streets. Surely we have been on this planet long enough to realize that rehabilitation doesn't really work.

- Rehabilitation is just a load of psychobabble that celebrities and socialist book-readers say to justify their public sector salaries. It is a waste of time to rehabilitate some criminals – they can't be helped.

- Some criminals are like animals. They don't belong in society, especially paedophiles. No matter how much we try to counsel these people, they have mental problems and cannot ever be allowed to re-enter society. God punished many people in the Bible so punishment must be the best solution. We need to be tough on crime.

No, criminals should be rehabilitated.

- Everyone has the possibility of rehabilitation. Every criminal can be rehabilitated, as a society we are not sophisticated enough to do this well. Paedophiles are locked up for now but one day we will know how to cure them through psychiatry. We are not dogs that have to be repeatedly beaten to enforce behavior patterns.

- Prisons are places where people learn how to be better criminals. Young lads who could be educated and put back in society get thrown inside with the worst criminals in society. Their standards drop, they become like their cellmates and they are educated in the tricks of crime and cheating. When they come out they often go straight into crime again because it's the only thing they know.

- The fear of punishment is not a good deterrent because criminals don't expect to be caught. Most people commit crime because they have suffered disadvantages in life, for example; coming from broken homes or being the victim of some extraordinary misfortune. Often people steal because they need to feed their families. This does not make them criminals. It makes them responsible family men.

- Punishment is negative, rehabilitation is positive; therefore rehab treats the cause, not the effect. Prevention is better than cure. The legal system is not a tool for taking revenge on people for the harm they've done. Make the most from a bad situation and rehabilitate who we can, to make them an example of the benefits of the system. We need to give criminals trade skills and allow the community to monitor them.

- Idle prisoners can be trained and educated to be useful people in society. They are an idle resource. If we can 'fix' a criminal, then we almost have a duty to do so. Punishment is only a temporary fix while the criminal is locked away. Simple punishment is wasteful and backward. Surely society has moved on from our vengeful past.

- People with drug problems really need rehabilitation and treatment. Punishment does not benefit them. Throwing addicts in prison is inhumane and ignorant of their condition. In New York, courts quickly identify drug users and put them under close supervision and give them long-term treatment, including mental health treatment, to break the cycle of drug abuse, addiction and crime. This is cost effective and humane.

- The more people we can release, the more we can lower costs. Prisons are expensive to run when you consider the hundreds of people, energy, manpower, etc, that are needed for years upon years. The money saved can be spent on more worthy causes than letting bad people rot without producing anything.

- Dostoevsky said, 'The degree of civilization in a society can be judged by entering its prisons.' If we still concentrate on punishing people then we have not moved forward since the Dark Ages. Modern society does not work best under fear. We cannot be taught as effectively through fear as we can through incentives. Rehabilitation gives people back their sense of pride and being.

Doing Time

Discuss as a class the fact that prisoners have a lot of time to think. What do they think about? What's a prison like from the inside? Do people feel guilty about their crimes? What pleasures can they enjoy? What positive things can prisoners do while in jail?

Now ask students to imagine that they have been sentenced to one-month's imprisonment. They should write a letter to their families explaining what it is like inside, talking about the crime they committed and telling them how they feel.

Vocab Refresh

Hardship – suffering, deprivation, oppression.

Rehab – in this context rehab means to restore the condition of virtue in a criminal's mind and behaviour.

Re-offend – to commit more criminal acts despite having been previously punished for doing so.

Remedies – solutions, in this context the headache of what to do with crims in society.

Potential criminals – a person who is not yet a criminal but is likely to become one through peer pressure, societal pressures, etc. A product of a broken home or society…

Pampering – overly well-treated and gratified – excessive indulgence, kindness or care.

Psychobabble – writing or talk using jargon from psychiatry or psychotherapy without particular accuracy or relevance.

Sophisticated – refined or developed in intellect and taste.

Paedophiles – an adult who is sexually attracted to a child or children.

Psychiatry – the practice or science of diagnosing and treating mental disorders.

Inhumane – lacking humanity, kindness, compassion, etc.

Dostoyevsky – Russian writer. His most famous works include Crime and Punishment and The Idiot. Dostoyevsky's writing explores tortuous lives in 19th century Russia.

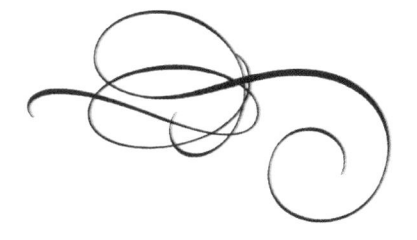

Debate 17 – Commerce & Culture

Debate 17 – Commerce & Culture

Are the businessperson and the manufacturer more important than the writer and the artist?

Goals of the Lesson

- For students to become more familiar with the relative value of producers in society.
- For students to practice debating, using persuasive devices and functional phrases.
- For students to find some form of consensus on the issue.

Rhetoric

Discuss and demonstrate these figures of speech with the class and explain that people who are able to speak forcefully and persuasively often use devices like this. Tell the students that you would like them to try and use these devices during the debate.

1. **Hyperbaton** – schemes featuring unusual or inverted word order.

'Why should their liberty than ours be more?'

2. **Hyperbole** – an exaggeration of a statement. Similar to **antiphrasis**. The opposite of **bathos, anticlimax, litotes, meiosis**.

'Will all great Neptune's ocean wash this blood
Clean from my hand? No. This my hand will rather
The multitudinous seas incarnadine,
Making the green one red.'
~ Shakespeare, *The Tragedy of Macbeth*

3. **Hypophora** – answering one's own rhetorical question at length.

'But there are only three hundred of us,' you object. Three hundred, yes, but men, but armed, but Spartans, but at Thermopylae: I have never seen three hundred so numerous.' ~ Seneca

Logical Fallacies

The Logical Fallacy is a rhetorical device which has no grounding in actual fact and is used by people to unfairly gain the upper hand in debates. Being able to spot such a flaw goes a long way to invalidating an opponent's argument.

1. **Least Plausible Hypothesis** – ignoring all of the most reasonable explanations. A violation of **Occam's Razor**.

'When I woke up my wallet was gone. A leprechaun must have taken it.'

Medical students are often told, "When you hear hoofbeats behind you, think horses, not zebras." Meaning don't overthink diagnosis – go for the simplest possibility first.

2. **Lies** – intentional **errors of fact**. The worst form of intellectual dishonesty.

'My colleagues, every statement I make today is backed up by sources, solid sources. These are not assertions. What we're giving you are facts and conclusions based on solid intelligence.' ~ Colin Powell in a speech to the UN prior to the Invasion of Iraq

3. **Meaningless Questions** – nonsensical thinking. Similar to **reifying**.

'How long is a piece of string?'

Preamble

This information is found on dozens of websites.

In considering this question it is necessary to bear in mind that businesspeople and manufacturers fall under the category of economic producers whereas artists and writers are cultural producers.

Economic Producers

George Stephenson (1781 – 1848) – The father of the railways, from Newcastle upon Tyne. Stephenson's ambition drove him to learn to read and write at night school. He then built several engines and for use at coal mines around the country. The pinnacle of these engines was *Rocket* which easily won the Rainhill Trials that inaugurated the Liverpool to Manchester Railway. Stephenson died an extremely wealthy man with interests in several mining, agricultural and engineering ventures. His son, Robert Stephenson was one of the finest civil engineers in the world.

Henry Ford (1863 – 1947) – In 1891, Ford became an engineer with the Edison Illuminating Company in Detroit. This event signified a conscious decision on Ford's part to dedicate his life to industrial pursuits. His promotion to Chief Engineer in 1893 gave him enough time and money to devote attention to his personal experiments on internal combustion engines.

The Ford Motor Company was incorporated in 1903. With the introduction of the Model T in 1908 Ford realized his dream of producing an automobile that was reasonably priced, reliable, and efficient. This vehicle initiated a new era in personal transportation. It was easy to operate, maintain, and handle on rough roads, immediately becoming a huge success.

To meet growing demand, the company opened a large factory in 1910. Here, Ford combined precision manufacturing, standardized and interchangeable parts, division of labour, and, in 1913, a continuous moving assembly line. This revolutionized automobile production by lowering costs. By 1918, half of all cars in America were Model Ts and Ford was the largest automobile manufacturer in the world.

Bill Gates (born 1955) – is the best-known entrepreneur of the personal computer revolution. Although he is admired by many, a large number of industry insiders criticize his business tactics, which they consider anti-competitive, an opinion which has in some cases been upheld by the courts. In the later stages of his career Gates has pursued a number of philanthropic endeavors, donating large amounts of money to various charitable organizations and scientific research programs through the Bill & Melinda Gates Foundation, established in 2000.

In 1975, before graduation Gates left Harvard to form Microsoft with his childhood friend Paul Allen. Gates soon became famous for his killer business deals. For example, he talked IBM into letting Microsoft retain the licensing rights to MS-DOS an operating system that IBM needed for their new personal computer. Gates proceeded to make a fortune from the licensing of MS-DOS.

<u>Cultural Producers</u>

Leonardo da Vinci (1452 – 1519) – the bastard son of a government official and a peasant woman. Da Vinci is the archetypal universal genius.

The Beatles – four working-class lads from Liverpool who grew up together and formed the band in 1960. Although their initial musical style was rooted in 1950s rock and roll and skiffle, the group worked with different musical genres, ranging from Tin Pan Alley to psychedelic rock. Their clothes, style and statements made them trend-setters while their growing social awareness saw their influence extend into the social and cultural revolutions of the 1960s. After the band broke up in 1970 all four members embarked upon successful solo careers.

Vaclav Havel (1936 – 2011) – was a Czech playwright, writer and politician. He was the tenth President of Czechoslovakia (1989 – 92) and the first President of the Czech Republic (1993 – 2003). He has written over twenty plays and numerous non-fiction works. He has received the US Presidential Medal of Freedom, the Philadelphia Liberty Medal, and the Ambassador of Conscience Award.

Beginning in the 1960s, his work turned to focus on the politics of Czechoslovakia. After the Prague Spring, he became increasingly active. In 1977, his involvement with the human rights manifesto *Charter 77* brought him international fame as the leader of the opposition in Czechoslovakia; it also led to his imprisonment. The 1989 'Velvet Revolution' launched Havel into the presidency. In this role he led Czechoslovakia and later the Czech Republic to multi-party democracy. His thirteen years in office saw radical change in his nation, including its split with Slovakia, which Havel opposed, its accession into NATO and start of the negotiations for membership in the European Union, which was completed in 2004.

Debating Phrases

<u>Challenges</u> – from Prime Minister's Questions

- He said that ….
- I've already to you that ….
- Don't you realize that ….
- Let me ask you one final time ….
- Let me tell you the real situation.
- What about ….

Fritillaria – Charles Rennie Mackintosh (1915)

Charles Rennie Mackintosh is in many ways a model cultural and economic producer. The Glasgow based businessman built a famed organization specializing in architecture, furniture, textiles and all types of household design. He was also a brilliant artist. Over his busy life Mackintosh amassed and lost a considerable fortune. He is responsible for much of the modernist design concepts which signify the early twentieth century.

The drawing typifies his minimalist, floral and distinctive chequered style. As with much of his work it is also influenced by the craving for Japanese culture which emerged in Europe after the Meiji Restoration at the end of the 19th century.

Great Debates

Businesspeople and manufacturers are more important than artists and writers.

- The activities of creating housing, growing food, providing us with the necessities of life, and the jobs we need to stay alive are all performed by the manufacturer and businessperson. If artists and writers cannot make a profit they are not worthy of enjoying the fruits of our labour. They should try to do something more beneficial to humanity.

- Artists and philosophers do not improve the world. Words are the freest things in the world and count for nothing in reality. Food on my table and clothes to wear are real things. Art and literature are non-essential fancy rubbish. If they disappeared we would still survive as a human race.

- Why should we admire people who don't do any real work? They encourage more people to bum around playing guitars and signing on the dole. This country needs to wake up and smell the coffee. Shakespeare is rubbish – who can understand what he wrote?

- We wouldn't have won the war without manufacturers and businesspeople however we could easily have won the war without artists and writers. Yes, writers talk about freedom and spirituality but they wouldn't be alive or free enough to talk about these things if someone had not have raised the standard of living and built an economy to allow them to flourish.

- Successful artists and writers make a lot of money but they don't contribute much to society outside of entertaining some folk. This is fundamentally unfair. They should be put to work by the state and be forced to give the profits to the poor. They should be forced to give some of their millions to charity.

- The most important people in society are coal miners because without them we would not have electricity or heat and they risk their lives every day for the good of society. Nurses are the next most important and they too get too little money. Creative people ought to live in the real world.

- The Industrial Revolution is the only reason we do not live like we did thousands of years ago. Philosophers talk a lot but they do not make the world a better place. Engineers do. Of course economic producers are more important than cultural producers.

Artists and writers are more important than businesspeople and manufacturers.

- For concepts like spirituality, freedom, questioning authority, etc, the artist is more important. Do you believe these things are important? If you don't you should try living in Nazi Germany.

^ from pacatrue.blogspot.com

- If we had more writers, we probably wouldn't have businesspeople with so much power. Business people actually have too much power and they are often bad for society. They exploit people and manipulate markets to serve their own interests. Business people are greedy, artists are generous.

- Businesspeople and manufacturers allow us to survive but artists and writers allow us to live. Where would we be without Shakespeare? Our culture would be poor, our expressions and ideas would not be as colourful and our lives would suffer as a result. It takes everyone to make the world. If you ask Bill Gates who is more important himself or Da Vinci, he would say Da Vinci.

- Writers and artists are businesspeople. They sell a product and work for a living. Shakespeare died an extremely wealthy man, the top chefs and designers are wealthy. Many artists do a lot of charity work. Taxpayers should support poor artists more because they contribute to the quality of our society. The creative industries create millions of jobs in developed countries.

- The freer a society is, the richer it is. This is a well-known fact in economics. If we give people to the freedom to follow their creative inspiration, everyone in society benefits. We wear better clothes than we used to, we listen to better music, we enjoy better entertainment therefore our quality of life is better. Quality of life is everything. What is the point in a life of working all day to make money but not being able to enjoy yourself with the fruits of creative people?

- Writers draw attention to the problems of the world. Without them there would be no journalists to blow the whistle on crimes, there would be no revolutions in history. Ideas are more important than money. Anyone can make money – that is the most basic life but few people can be writers or artists. We need to respect talented people who communicate well rather than simply trade a product.

- The Renaissance and the Enlightenment were artistic and intellectual movements that improved the state of mankind. In China, Confucius and Buddha were responsible for civilizing the people. Religion is generally a civilizing influence. Businesspeople given total freedom would simply destroy the planet and cheat everyone on earth for their own benefit. Paper shuffling and earth-raping are not more important than expression and enlightenment.

Dear Editor

Ask students to write a letter to *The Guardian* complaining about the lack of respect and government funding for artists in their country. They should outline the consequences for economic growth and provide some solutions.

Vocab Refresh

Philosopher – someone who spends a large proportion of his day staring into the bottom of a beer glass.

Bum around – to behave in a work-shy manner, bumming drinks and cigarettes of people, borrowing money, lying around watching TV all day.

Signing on the dole – claiming unemployment benefits.

Admire – to respect and look to someone.

Spirituality – the nature of being introspective, thoughtful and sensitive.

Manipulate markets – to artificially interfere, by restricting supply to raise prices, or flooding the market with a product to drive down prices and put people out of business, fixing prices in collusion with other firms and various other speculative and anti-competitive practices.

Blow the whistle – to alert and inform the general public or powers that be about a crime.

The Renaissance – Intellectual movement and 'rediscovering' of the classical texts beginning in Italy in the 14th century and spreading to Northern Europe by the 16th century.

The Enlightenment – An intellectual movement beginning in the mid-eighteenth century in which the freedom and rights of mankind were affirmed.

Confucius – a seminal Chinese sage who lived around the same time as the Buddha and Socrates. His influence continues prominently in Asian culture today.

Paper shuffling – a metonym for conducting business in the manner or pen-pushing, bureaucratic or administrative or clerical work.

Earth-raping – exploiting resources with zero payback to the local population.

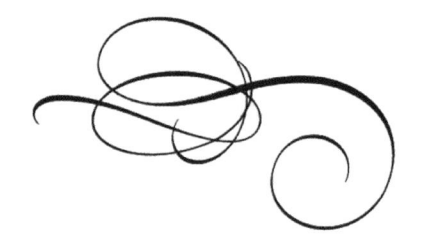

Debate 18 – Adoption

Debate 18 – Adoption

Should a same sex couple in a stable, loving relationship, be excluded from the possibility of child adoption?

Goals of the Lesson

- For students to become more familiar with concepts and terminology related to homosexuality.
- For students to practice debating, using persuasive devices and functional phrases.
- For students to find some form of consensus on the issue.

Rhetoric

Discuss and demonstrate these figures of speech with the class and explain that people who are able to speak forcefully and persuasively often use devices like this. Tell the students that you would like them to try and use these devices during the debate.

1. **Hysteron proteron** – the inversion of the usual temporal or causal order between two elements. Similar to **hyperbaton** and **anastrophe**.

'I'm going to kill that magician. I'll dismember him and then I'll sue him.' ~ Woody Allen, *New York Stories*

2. **Innuendo** – a hidden meaning in a sentence that makes sense whether it is detected or not.

'Lesbos is one the best bird watching spots in Europe.'

3. **Irony** – use of word in a way that conveys a meaning opposite to its usual meaning. Also see **antiphrasis, oxymoron** and **paradiastole**.

'Gentlemen, you can't fight in here! This is the War Room.' ~ *Dr Strangelove*

The baseball 'World Series' is only played by teams from the US and Canada.

Logical Fallacies

The Logical Fallacy is a rhetorical device which has no grounding in actual fact and is used by people to unfairly gain the upper hand in debates. Being able to spot such a flaw goes a long way to invalidating an opponent's argument.

1. **Misunderstanding the Nature of Statistics.**

President Dwight Eisenhower expressed astonishment and alarm on discovering that fully half of all Americans had below average intelligence. – from Carl Sagan's *The Fine Art of Baloney Detection*

2. **Moving the Goalposts** – dismissing and altering the terms of the argument / adding new rules. If an arguer does this enough times, he will eventually accrue enough advantages and increase the chances that his opponent will make a slip. Sometimes it's best for a magnanimous arguer to allow this as a face-saving **escape hatch**.

If you are asked to provide just one example, and you do, but your opponent asks for further ones.

Barack Obama's birth certificate is a good example.

3. **Needling** – *ad hominem* and other devices designed to anger your opponent such as interrupting, clowning, noise, insults, and other delaying tactics.

Preamble

From Wikipedia.

Many lesbian, gay, bisexual, and transgendered people are parents. In the 2000 U.S. Census, 33 percent of female same-sex couple households and 22 percent of male same-sex couple households reported at least one child under the age of 18 living in the home. Nevertheless, LGBT parenting in general, and adoption by LGBT couples in particular, are issues of major political controversy in many Western countries, often seen as part of a 'culture war' between conservatives and social liberals. Common methods of LGBT parenting are adoption, donor insemination, foster parenting, and surrogacy, as well as parenting by a mother or father who was previously in a heterosexual relationship. As of 2005, an estimated 270,313 children in the United States live in households headed by same-sex couples.

The Church of Jesus Christ of Latter-day Saints argues for traditional gender roles in parenting, claiming they are foundational to parenting. Based on research showing that, on average, children do best when raised by their biological parents in a low-conflict marriage, some argue that legal marriage is a way of encouraging monogamy and commitment by those who may create children through their sexual coupling. One prominent supporter of this viewpoint, syndicated columnist Maggie Gallagher, argues that 'babies are most likely to grow to functioning adulthood when they have the care and attention of both their mother and their father.' Focus on the Family points to academic studies which state that children raised with both parents, as opposed to children raised by single mothers, increase children's cognitive and verbal skills, academic performance, involvement in or avoidance of high-risk behaviors and crime, and emotional and psychological health. However, another study has held that being without a resident father from infancy does not seem to have negative consequences for children.

Research has found no major differences in parenting or child development between families headed by two mothers and other fatherless families. However research has also shown children raised by single mothers or children raised by two mothers perceived themselves to be less cognitively and physically competent than their peers from father-present families. Children without fathers had more interactions, severe disputes and depended more on their mothers. Sons showed more feminine but no less masculine characteristics of gender role behavior. Compared with young adults who had single mothers, men and women raised by two mothers were slightly more likely to consider the possibility of having a same-sex partner, and more of them had been involved in at least a brief same-sex relationship, but there was no statistical difference in sexual identity of children compared to children of opposite-sex parents.

A number of health and child-welfare organizations 'support the parenting of children by lesbians and gay men, and condemn attempts to restrict competent, caring adults from serving as foster and/or adoptive parents.' Noted Harvard political philosopher and legal scholar John Rawls supports gay marriage and does not believe that it would undermine the welfare of children.

Same-sex marriage opponents argue that mainstream health and mental health organizations have, in many cases, taken public positions on homosexuality and same-sex marriage that are based on their own social and political views rather than the available science.

Debating Phrases

<u>Challenging</u> – from Prime Minister's Questions

- Answer the question!
- Now the fact of the matter is ….
- The reason why ….
- If you are saying that ….
- Are you honestly saying ….
- I would put it a little bit differently.

Tending Children at the Orphanage in Haarlem – Jan de Bray (1663)

De Bray was a Dutch master who made several baroque paintings of and for Haarlem orphans. He himself lost much of his family in the Plague.

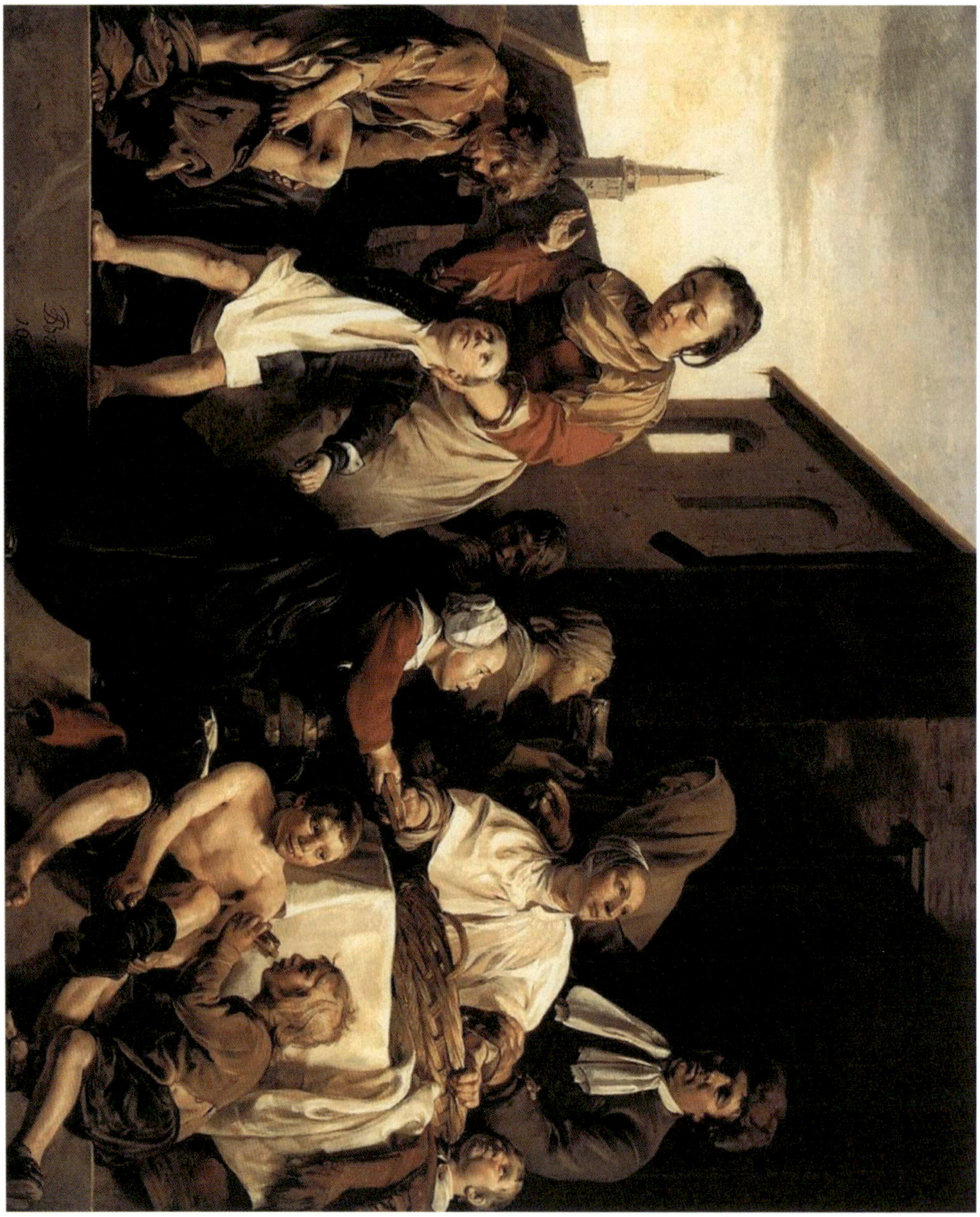

Yes, same sex couples should be allowed to have kids.

- Society is changing. The traditional nuclear family with a married mum and dad is no longer the only acceptable way. Many countries now give legal rights to gay couples because they see that gay relationships are stable. Human beings are human beings – who cares if they are gay? Sexuality is only a small part of a person's life.

- Nature shows that in many animals, when one or both parents die, an uncle or aunt often takes on the child-rearing role. The child is an individual and is not going to become strange or gay just because his guardians are. People, even children, can think for themselves. Kids don't need to worry about sexuality until they are teenagers. By that time they have worked out for themselves if they like boys or girls. Parenting has nothing to do with it.

- I know several same-sex couples in stable, loving relationships who would make much better parents than I would. Sexuality is a private matter and should not affect how good someone is at being a parent. The question of whether someone is gay or straight is irrelevant. It is not anyone's business to say that being gay is right or wrong. People should live and let live.

- Babies are born with their sexuality already decided and their upbringing will not affect this. An adopted child has different genes from its parents. Even related children are very often completely different to their parents. We should not worry that children adopted by gay parents will also become gay.

- Homophobia is wrong, and must be fought everywhere. Not long ago homosexuals were sent to prison in many countries. If we can be so wrong in our attitudes, can we also be wrong in not allowing gays to adopt a child? If we really want to move forward and become a modern society, gay adoption should not be a problem.

- Who cares if children do become gay anyway? Shouldn't we be able to live alongside gays and treat them equally in our society? Shouldn't we even encourage people to admit being gay? What's wrong with it? Kids should be proud that their parents are gay and live perfectly normal lives.

- Gay adoption is better than having a child grow up in an orphanage with no loving parents at all. These days too many children don't have good stable families. People who say homosexuality is bad are ignorant bigots who are living in the past. They are no different to racists. Homosexuality harms no one.

No, same sex couples should not be allowed kids.

- Evolution and nature show that natural development of the young is helped by a heterosexual couple. The nuclear family is an ideal family. I don't really think it's natural for a child to be brought up missing a gender in his / her parenting. It could retard the child's social skills with girls or boys because they have not had experience of interacting with that sex at home.

- Research in the US (Univ. of Illinois Law Review, 1997) says that children raised in homosexual households are much more likely to be gay themselves. This is bad for society in the long term. It will mean smaller populations. This will mean that our country will become poorer and less powerful.

- Allowing adoption by gay couples will encourage unnatural upbringing. It is unfair on the child. All children need both male and female role models. If they don't have a father they are more likely to cause trouble – both boys and girls. If girls don't have a father they may have difficulty making relationships with men – the same is true of boys with no mother. Gay adoption has the potential to cause serious problems in society.

- Homophobic language and behaviour is still common in society. Placing a young child who does not have an opinion of their own, in the care of a gay couple exposes them to this prejudice and subjects them to ridicule or violence. Whatever ideal we might have, the psychological and physical welfare of the child must come first.

- Men in this world need to do masculine things like fix cars, get into trouble, drink beer and chase girls. This should be taught by the father. Boys who grow up in a gay household will never learn to be real men. They will not be able to communicate how they feel during puberty and their parents will not be able to understand them. This is not good parenting.

- The Bible says homosexuality is evil. God created Adam and Eve. The problem is that gay parents are destroying the social and moral fabric of this world. The traditional social unit is the family with a mom and a dad. Why should we go against centuries of social norms?

- Bringing a heterosexual child up in a gay household gives them a distorted view of minority sexuality. A girl brought up by two men would not get the benefit from a feminine influence. The girl would have no one to relate to. It would be difficult for her to learn about women's issues and feelings. This would put her at a serious disadvantage in life. Her schoolmates would also probably tease her and think she is strange. She would then see herself as strange. This could lead to depression and suicide.

Several of these points are taken from debatepedia.idebate.org/en/index.php/Debate:_Gay_adoption

Great Debates

Gay Rights

Have students in pairs create a charter outlining the rights of gays and lesbians in their countries. Change partners and present the charter to the new partner who is a judge. Discuss which of the points on each charter is acceptable or not.

Things to consider:

Freedom to marry.
Freedom to raise children.
Freedom to work in any job, without discrimination and bullying.
Freedom from religious intolerance.
Respect in society.
Education about homosexuality in schools.
Condemnation of societies and people intolerant of homosexuality.
Hate speech laws brought into force.
Promotion of gay culture and lifestyle by government and media.
Affirmative action for gay people.

Vocab Refresh

Child-rearing – the business of raising children.

Same-sex couples – opposite of 'straight' couples.

Irrelevant – not important, of no value to the issue.

Bigot – ignorant person who hates a group of people, based on their beliefs or harmless behaviours.

Heterosexual couple – opposite of a gay couple.

The nuclear family – the opposite of an extended family. Two parents + children.

To retard – to hold back, especially in a sense of educational / cognitive development.

Upbringing – childhood, raising, nurturing, educational background, social environment.

Role model – a person who younger children can admire and aspire to.

Heterosexual – a person who is sexually attracted to a members of the opposite sex.

Distorted – misshapen or twisted view of reality / the world.

Feminine – female-like.

Masculine – male.

Homophobic – anti-gay.

Prejudice – intolerant dislike of a group of people.

Moral fabric – the shared moral values of a group.

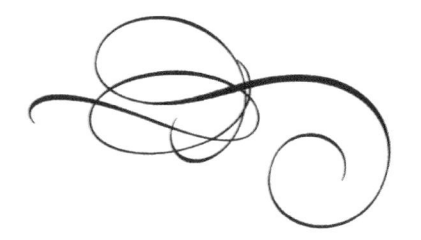

Debate 19 – Social Order

Debate 19 – Social Order

'In a civilized society, we must always have people above to be obeyed & people below to be commanded.' Is this true?

Goals of the Lesson

- For students to become more familiar with the concepts of elitism and egalitarianism in society.
- For students to practice debating, using persuasive devices and functional phrases.
- For students to find some form of consensus on the issue.

Rhetoric

Discuss and demonstrate these figures of speech with the class and explain that people who are able to speak forcefully and persuasively often use devices like this. Tell the students that you would like them to try and use these devices during the debate.

1. **Isocolon** – use of usually terse parallel structures of the same length in successive clauses.

'They have suffered severely, but they have fought well.' ~ Winston Churchill

'I speak Spanish to God, Italian to women, French to men, and German to my horse.' ~ Charles V

2. **Internal rhyme** – using two or more rhyming words in the same sentence.

I am the daughter of Earth and Water,
And the nursling of the Sky;
I pass through the pores of the ocean and shores;
I change, but I cannot die.
~ Percy Bysshe Shelley, *The Cloud*

3. **Litotes** – emphasizing the magnitude of a statement by denying its opposite.

'You're not wrong.'

Logical Fallacies

The Logical Fallacy is a rhetorical device which has no grounding in actual fact and is used by people to unfairly gain the upper hand in debates. Being able to spot such a flaw goes a long way to invalidating an opponent's argument.

1. **Non Sequitur** – something that just does not follow.

'If you buy this car your family will be safer.' – While some cars are safer than others, they will most likely decrease instead of increase your family's overall safety.

2. **Not Invented Here** – ideas from elsewhere are made unwelcome. Similar to **Wisdom of the Ancients** (appeal to tradition) and **xenophobia**.

'This is the way we've always done it.'

'If you don't like it then go and live elsewhere [insert Country X].'

3. **Outdated Information** – a form of intellectual dishonesty. Information is given, but it is not the latest information on the subject.

Some creationists like to quote old scientific articles from the 1950s which have subsequently been disproved.

It was once argued that medical testing of penicillin on animals was unethical as it was toxic to hamsters / rabbits, etc. However, it is now established that this is not the case.

Preamble

From Wikipedia.

Elitism is the belief that a select group of people with outstanding personal abilities, intellect, wealth, specialized training or experience, or other distinctive attributes are those whose views are to be taken the most seriously or carry the most weight; whose views and actions are most likely to be constructive to society as a whole; or whose extraordinary skills, abilities or wisdom render them especially fit to govern. Members of the upper classes are sometimes known as the elite.

Elites may grant themselves extra privileges at the expense of others. This form of elitism may be described as discrimination. Additionally, the 'elite' often possess little practical knowledge of what they profess. They may hold the belief that they are above the rules that apply to the masses. The 'Do as I Say, Don't Do as I Do.' and 'Its Not My Fault' are core beliefs that lead them through life with little or no accountability for their actions. A view of self worth drives their view of the world and those in it. Elitist people or groups believe they are better than the rest of society, and therefore put themselves before others.

Elitism endorses the exclusion of large numbers of people from positions of privilege or power. Thus, many activists and politicians seek the social equality of **egalitarianism**, populism, socialism, or communism. They may also support affirmative action, social security, luxury taxes, and increasingly high progressive taxes for the wealthiest members of society. All of these measures seek to reduce the gap of power between the elite and the ordinary.

Pluralism is the belief that public policy decisions should be (or, descriptively, are) the result of the struggle of forces exerted by large populations (workers, consumers, retirees, parents, etc.) directly or indirectly in the policy-making process. This is contrasted with elitism which is the belief that decisions should be (or are being) made essentially according to the interests or ideas of elites.

Feudalism

The social and economic system which characterized most European societies in the Middle Ages goes by the name of feudalism. Every man knew his place and was a servant of his lord. Feudalism was a society in which every man was bound to every other by mutual ties of loyalty and service. Feudal society was characterized by military landholders and working peasants. The nobility included bishops, for the church was one of the greatest of medieval landowners. Near the bottom of the social pyramid were the agricultural laborers, or villeins, and beneath them, the serfs.

Fascism

The Nazis employed a concept called *Führerprinzip* which was used by the German army and by German society as a whole. Every leader would have absolute responsibility for their own area and answer to no-one except their superiors. Subordinates must show absolute obedience. Military organizations still use a similar principle to this day because it is efficient and can harness great synergies. In practice though, *Führerprinzip* often led to micromanagement and an inability to formulate coherent policy.

Tall Poppy Syndrome

Tall Poppy Syndrome is a term used in Australia, New Zealand and Canada, in which the majority have a desire to punish the successful. Someone is a target of tall poppy syndrome when his or her assumption of a higher economic, social, or political position is criticized as being presumptuous, attention seeking, or without merit.

This phenomenon is often interpreted as resulting from resentment and envy of others' success. On the other side of the coin, however, such critics see themselves, not as envious, but as justly deflating the pretensions of those who take themselves too seriously or flaunt their success without due humility. Apparent cases of tall poppy syndrome are thus often explained as resentment not of *success* but of snobbery and arrogance. Those whose approach to success is seen as suitably humble can escape.

Critics of the tall poppy syndrome sometimes declare that the United States is relatively free of tall poppy attitudes. Americans are thought to appreciate the successful, seeing them as an example to admire and attempt to emulate. In the cultures of the UK and Commonwealth nations, such commentators assert, many resent success of their fellows.

Debating Phrases

<u>Challenges</u> – from Prime Minister's Questions

- The big question is ….
- You know it's true.
- Do you accept that ….
- Let us be clear about what this is.
- I have to say ….

Pyramid of Capitalism (1911)

This cartoon was printed in *The Industrial Worker*, an American magazine. Capitalism is here cynically depicted as an extension of a feudal order. The picture was produced at a pre-welfare state era when the West was struggling to cope with large, urbanized and impoverished working-class populations and Marxist ideas were gaining a lot of ground.

CAPITALISM
WE RULE YOU
WE FOOL YOU
WE SHOOT AT YOU
WE EAT FOR YOU
WE WORK FOR ALL
WE FEED ALL
PYRAMID OF CAPITALIST SYSTEM
INDUSTRIAL WORKER
Industrial Unionism
Published in the English Language
ISSUED BY NEDELJKOVICH, BRASHICH AND KUHARICH

Yes, in civilized society we must have people above to be obeyed and people below to be commanded.

- If I am in the army and someone needs to say 'go', the others must go. It is likely that we will all die without this. Command and obey is a survival strategy that benefits the group. Without it, evolution would not happen and we would not exist. This is a law of nature.

^ pacatrue.blogspot.com

- It is true that all men are created equal but some are more equal than others. Some people are not intelligent (intellectually or emotionally) enough to lead others. Some people do not have the ability to make things happen in organizations. It is through teamwork that mankind achieves things and teams need leaders. Society is basically one big team so of course we need people to lead and people to follow.

- Confucianism teaches that we should have unquestioning obedience towards our superiors. This creates a harmonious and orderly society. Humanity has developed from primitive beginnings by being organized into hierarchies. This is of course natural. In nature only the strongest can survive. This is the only efficient way.

- Who is going to do all the low paid jobs if everyone refuses to be commanded? Who is going to do all the hard manual work? Who is going to fight in the army? If people have a choice, they won't do it. We need an educated elite to control the economy while the masses do the hard work. This is how ants work and ants are the most successful animals in the history of Earth.

- In the old days, the fear of God stopped people from stealing and killing all the time because people believed they would go to hell if they did. America was settled by god-fearing farmers who worked hard because they believed it would save their soul in heaven. This proves that is it necessary for people to obey a higher power. Especially because there are so many simple uneducated people in the world, it is important that the clever people can do the difficult thinking for them.

- Rich and powerful countries like Great Britain have had an aristocracy for hundreds and hundreds of years and they controlled most of the world at one time. Britain still continues to work as a wealthy and fair society. Mutinies were not tolerated at all in the British Empire and rightly so.

- Leaders are born, not made. The masses are usually jealous of achievers. It's best to live in a competitive society. A competitive society is a civilized society because the best people get to the top. There will be always be simple, lowly people but they should have the opportunity to work for the bigger people so they can prove what talents they might have and climb out from their position.

- Plato said that the best form of government was rule by a small group of philosophers because only the cleverest could know what is best for the state. We should respect experts and follow their advice and policies. This is practical and sensible. If everyone has a say in government, we would have chaos.

No, we should not always have people being obeyed and commanded in civilized society.

- Is there is a permanent group of people who are commanders with others simply to serve them? No. We are not living in feudal times. All men are created equal – although not equal in abilities, we are all created with equal rights and that is the only truly fair society.

- In an emergency, people need to be obeyed but when those in charge try to make every thing into an emergency so that they can stay in power... – that is hardly civilized behaviour. It is natural for leaders to abuse their power in this way because *power corrupts and absolute power corrupts absolutely.*

^ Iconoclast421 – anythingexceptthetruth.blogspot.com

- Yes, people naturally organize themselves into hierarchies of power, but this is by no means a qualification for civilized societies. Instead, a truly 'civilized' society would be one where everyone is equal. The first countries to do this were the USA and France after their democratic revolutions at the end of 18th century.

- People need to think for themselves. Questioning authority is healthy. The fear of god made us primitive and kept us there. A freer a society is a richer society. Hopefully, in the future we will live in a truly civilized 'flat world' where everyone has the same opportunities in life. Surely this is the best future for mankind? Feudalism and slavery were common when the world was not as civilized as it is now. Thank god these terrible institutions have gone.

- The leaders answer to no one. Everyone should be accountable for their actions otherwise we have dictatorship. Everyone, even the rulers, must be subject to the same law. This is the only way we can guarantee a stable, fair and wealthy society. It's bad for morale if a small group of people rule the masses, even if they do know better. Majority unity is better for morale and general public happiness.

- In Australia people say that "Tall poppies get their heads chopped off." which means that no one is better than anyone else. Australia is the world's most equal society and it is also one of the best places in the world to live. This is no coincidence. Arrogant and self-important people have no place in a truly civilized society where people have respect for each other.

- Elitism is not my definition of 'civilized'. Command / obedience = subjugation. Why do you have to subjugate and threaten people in a civilized society? Why would you talk about 'above' and 'below' if everyone were fully respected? I call this primitive thinking.

- I had to attend a poorly-funded school and my father was a wage worker and made a minimum wage. Why should I be denied opportunities for the rest of my live just because of the situation I was born into? I have skills to offer the country but I am not given the chance to. Clearly, a level playing field benefits the whole country.

The CV of a Great Leader

Ask each student to think of his or her favourite leader. These could be from politics, the arts, sports, business or history. Based on some research, each student should write a curriculum vitae for that person. Why they were such good leaders? What personal qualities did they have? How did they lead? What did they achieve? What do they wish to achieve next?

Vocab Refresh

Confucianism – the teachings of the ancient Chinese sage and proto-teacher, Kong Zi.

Primitive – basic, rudimentary and lacking in all refinement and sophistication.

Hierarchies – natural pyramids of order and power found in nature, society and commerce.

Aristocracy – a small group of landowners who earn from rents and rule via hereditary succession.

Mutiny – uprising among armed forces in which the ruling officers are executed by the rank and file and the existing order is replaced.

Achievers – people who attain goals and represent success in human life.

Chaos – the opposite of 'order'. Utter confusion with random, unpredictable events.

Feudal – an old social system where by peasants or slaves would perpetually survive on subsistence means while their overlords reaped a large percentage of their production.

to Corrupt – to slowly destroy and erode the virtue of something.

Elitism – advocacy of rule by a small band of powerful individuals.

to Subjugate – to bring a group of people under control and domination. To conquer and master.

Institutions – a well-established organization or set of relationships that is accepted as a fundamental part of a culture, such as marriage: *the institution of the family.*

Morale – group spirit.

Coincidence – a striking occurrence of two or more events at one time apparently by mere chance.

Arrogant – making claims or pretensions to superior importance or rights; overbearingly assuming; insolently proud.

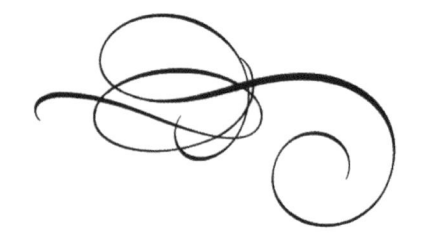

Debate 20 – Military Interventionism

Debate 20 – Military Interventionism

Is military action that defies international law is sometimes justified?

Goals of the Lesson

- For students to become more familiar with the concepts and ethical basis of taxation.
- For students to practice debating, using persuasive devices and functional phrases.
- For students to find some form of consensus on the issue.

Rhetoric

Discuss and demonstrate these figures of speech with the class and explain that people who are able to speak forcefully and persuasively often use devices like this. Tell the students that you would like them to try and use these devices during the debate.

1. **Malapropism** – using a word through confusion with a word that sounds similar.

'… my knight in white satin armour.'
'Quasimodo predicted this'
'Create a little dysentery among the ranks'
The Sopranos

'I might just fade into Bolivian, you know what I mean?' ~ Mike Tyson

2. **Meiosis** – use of understatement, usually to diminish the importance of something.

'The Troubles' as a name for decades of violence in Northern Ireland.

3. **Merism** – referring to a whole by enumerating some of its parts. This may be found in legal language, especially archaic legalese, in order to cover all angles in a contract. A **circumlocution**.

'I searched high and low.'

'I bequeath, convey, and devise the rest, residue, and remainder of my property, whether real or personal, and wheresoever it may be situated, to. . . .'

Logical Fallacies

The Logical Fallacy is a rhetorical device which has no grounding in actual fact and is used by people to unfairly gain the upper hand in debates. Being able to spot such a flaw goes a long way to invalidating an opponent's argument.

1. **Pious Fraud** – a fraud or a **lie** done to accomplish some good end, on the theory that the end justifies the means. More generally, it is when an emotionally committed speaker makes an claim that is knowingly incorrect.

British Prime Minister Tony Blair was accused in 2003 of 'sexing up' his evidence that Iraq had Weapons of Mass Destruction.

2. **Poisoning the Wells** – discrediting the sources used by your opponent. A type of **genetic fallacy**. This stems from the medieval European myth that the Black Plague was caused by Jews poisoning town wells. <u>This argument is particularly relevant in today's debate.</u>

'Before turning the floor over to my opponent, I ask you to remember that those who oppose my plans do not have the best wishes of the company at heart.' ~ from Nizkor.org

3. **Psychogenetic Fallacy** – blaming the arguer's position on the psychological reason for his believing it. A personal attack.

'You only offer that opinion because it is what you were taught in school. You were brainwashed.'

'You only believe in God because you were an alcoholic and suffered from depression. God is an emotional crutch to get you through life.'

Preamble

From Wikipedia.

Pre-emptive Wars and are started in order to gain the advantage of *initiative* and to harm the enemy at a moment of minimal protection. However, article 51 of the UN Charter states that self-defence is restricted to a response to an armed attack. Examples of pre-emptive actions:

1. German invasions of Denmark & Norway (1940) – Germany argued that Britain might have used them as launching points for an attack, or prevented supply of strategic materials to Germany.

2. British and Soviet invasion of Iran (1941) secured a supply corridor into Russia. The Shah of Iran appealed to President Franklin D. Roosevelt to intervene, but was rebuffed on the grounds that "movements of conquest by Germany will [if given the opportunity] continue and will extend beyond Europe to Asia, Africa, and even to the Americas, unless they are stopped by military force."

3. Nazi invasion of Russia (Operation Barbarossa) in 1941 is usually considered an aggressive war that started with a surprise attack on a former ally. Hitler's apologist, David Irving, in his book Hitler's War controversially argued that this was a preventative war.

4. Japan v USA (1941) – though normally considered an act of aggression by Japan, apologists for Imperial Japan have argued that this war was preventative.

5. The Six-Day War (1967) – The Israel Defence Forces, fearing Arab military build-ups on its border, famously launched a devastating pre-emptive strike on Arab forces.

6. The United States attack and invasion of Iraq and Afghanistan are recent examples of pre-emptive War.

Ideologies

Neo-conservativism

This position supports using American economic and military power to bring liberalism, democracy, and human rights to other countries. Characteristics include:

- a tendency to see the world in binary good/evil terms
- low tolerance for diplomacy
- readiness to use military force
- emphasis on US unilateral action
- disdain for multilateral organizations
- focus on the Middle East

George W Bush laid out his neoconservative vision of the future in January 2002, following the September 11 attacks. The speech named Iraq, Iran and North Korea as an "axis of evil" and "pose a grave and growing danger." Bush suggested the possibility of preemptive war: "I will not wait on events, while dangers gather. I will not stand by, as peril draws closer and closer. The United States of America will not permit the world's most dangerous regimes to threaten us with the world's most destructive weapons."

Retired General William Odom, who served under Ronald Reagan, was openly critical of Neoconservative influence in the Bush Administration, saying: "It's pretty hard to imagine us going into Iraq without the strong lobbying efforts from the neocons, who think they know what's good for Israel more than Israel knows."

The Bush Doctrine of preemptive war was explicitly stated in the National Security Council text National Security Strategy of the United States, published September, 2002. "We must deter and defend against the threat before it is unleashed... even if uncertainty remains as to the time and place of the enemy's attack... The United States will, if necessary, act preemptively." The Bush Doctrine was greeted with accolades by many neoconservatives.

Critics take issue with neoconservatives' support for aggressive foreign policy. Critics from the left take issue with what they characterize as unilateralism and lack of concern with international consensus through organizations such as the United Nations. Neoconservatives respond by describing their shared view as a belief that national security is best attained by actively promoting freedom and democracy abroad as in the democratic peace theory through the support of pro-democracy movements, foreign aid and in certain cases military intervention.

There were also controversies with Venezuelan president Hugo Chavez saying the USA plotted to overthrow his presidency. Both Bolivia and Venezuela accused the George W. Bush administration of interfering with their democratically elected governments. There are further controversies with earlier CIA activities in the Americas.

Neoliberalism

The Obama administration could be considered the polar opposite of neo-conservatism. Its instincts are multilateralism, being committed, for example, to adhering to the Kyoto Protocol and to international agreements like the Geneva Convention. It places a high priority on diplomacy, with Obama being open to direct talks with long-ignored countries like Iran and Cuba. Military intervention is genuinely considered to be the last option.

Political Realism / Realpolitik

This predicts that conflict should be the norm in international relations. Machiavelli was the first philosopher to illustrate the concepts within realism. Consider some of his quotes:

'A prince should never neglect what should be done for what ought to be done.'
'A prince should think of nothing but war.'
'A wise ruler ought never to keep faith when by doing so it would be against his interests.'
'Hatred is gained as much by good works as by evil.'
'Hence it comes about that all armed Prophets have been victorious, and all unarmed Prophets have been destroyed.'
'It is better to be feared than loved, if you cannot be both.'
'The fact is that a man who wants to act virtuously in every way necessarily comes to grief among so many who are not virtuous.'
'There is no avoiding war; it can only be postponed to the advantage of others.'

Idealism

This was the policy adopted by the USA following The First World War. It was argued that war is mutually destructive and co-operation and peace are the only way forward in international relations.

Utilitarianism

A philosophy expounded by John Stuart Mill in which every action which occurs in society should ultimately benefit the people as a whole. Therefore in this context, military intervention which is for the greater good of humanity or regional or even national humanity is justified in a utilitarian calculus of moral worth and overall happiness from the eventual outcome. The opposite of this philosophy is virtue ethics which focuses on character and the consequences of actions are not considered.

Debating Phrases

<u>Challenges</u> – from Prime Minister's Questions

- I think, if I may so, that ….
- In the context of ….
- I've just got to ask you, ….
- Let's look at the facts again.
- X says, and I quote ….

The Signing of the First Geneva Convention – Charles Édouard Armand-Dumaresq (1864)

The Geneva Convention comes from a long line of momentous international treaties established by European elite power brokers for the purpose of ending or dealing with the effects of wars. In total there have been four Geneva Conventions, the final one in 1949 being ratified by 194 countries. Switzerland, being arguably the most pacifist country in the world, was an appropriate place to make a deal of such importance in defining how war should be conducted. That is, in a civilized way.

Great Debates

Yes, military action that defies international law is sometimes justified.

- Yes, military action against international law is justified if it for the greater good. If, for example, it is to protect a weak country from an aggressive neighbour. Such action is especially necessary against terrorists. If only someone could have invaded Germany before 1939, we would have avoided WW2 and millions of deaths.

- If the bad guys don't respect international law, why should the good guys when we need to stop the bad guys? We have to go out and stop the terrorists overseas. We have to be the global policeman. The world is a mess and we need to get serious about dealing with it. The danger is not that military action is against international law, the danger is that the action we take will not be enough.

- Sometimes emergencies require swift action without political delays. Perhaps there could be a humanitarian disaster and millions of innocent people could die as a result. In this situation, breaking international law is a good thing. Following international law would make the country a bigger criminal if they deliberately stand back and look the other way.

- Sometimes a country has to attack another country to establish permanent peace in the region. Even if this breaks international law, it benefits the whole region in the long run. We have to look at the bigger picture and take a long term view. There have been countless historical examples where this has happened. Countries have intervened in other countries' business time and time again. Why should we change now?

- Just because the West is "morally bankrupt" does not mean that the bad guys are not bad guys and should not be punished. It's better to be pragmatic than to be led by inflexible ideology. Successful countries deal with problems as they happen and are not bound by theory or outdated principles. There will always be bad countries – this is not the time for the good countries to become weak.

- The use of force by the international community in places like Kosovo, East Timor, Haiti and Somalia was an important part of building peace in the 1990s. These interventions helped end humanitarian disasters in which the stronger side viciously abused the human rights (and worse) of their weaker enemies.

- Who is to say what is right and wrong? We can't let weak liberals or other governments dictate how the world should be run. They don't know the real issues most of the time, or they have some business interests with the bad guys. Failure to act on a bad country shows apathy. Some people care more than others – they are the ones who take an active leadership role to right the world's wrongs.

- Just because we don't follow international law doesn't mean everybody else can break it too. That's a *tu quoque* argument. If the Americans had intervened earlier in WW2 we would have saved a lot of trouble. The policy of isolation is bad for everyone and cowardly.

No, military action that defies international law is never justified.

- If there needs to be any military action, international law should probably be changed. The beauty of the UN is that it is democratic; no one country has complete say. We solve far more problems in the world by discussing and reaching agreement than going off by ourselves and using force. War is the ultimate failure of diplomacy.

- Military intervention almost always means a strong country going against a weak country, which is always unfair. Military intervention is simply international bullying. Governments who consider intervention are, by nature, military-centered, unilateralist and overreaching. This is not a healthy thing for the international community.

- One man's terrorist is another man's freedom fighter. Who is to say what is right and wrong – the most powerful? Surely not. Unilateralism shows lack of respect for the world community. Eventually the world will lack respect for the unilateral power. What right has anyone got to intervene in a foreign country's business?

- If some don't respect international law what's the point in having international law? It becomes useless and we may as well allow the powerful to rule as they wish. Where do you draw the line? If the most powerful don't respect the law, they are a bad example to everyone else. No one will respect international law and we will go back to anarchy. The rule of law is the most important factor in development of a healthy society and civilization. It must be respected above everything else.

- It might be justified but it is still illegal. Force is disgusting. We should live in a world of peace. How can countries go around saying everyone should respect international when they don't themselves? They are hypocrites. The foreign policy of military interventionism has brought death and destruction to many foreign lands.

- Obviously, rules aren't always perfect, so unless international law is extremely lax, there may be some actions that are justified that defy international law. The problem is that international law is not strong to begin with. It's not easy to bring every single country together. If international law is seen as something to be broken whenever necessary, then there is really no international law at all. We need to strengthen international law so everyone respects it. This is the best future for our world.

- Hindsight is a great thing, but we do not have the luxury of it. Nobody knows who the real bad guys are – we often go after the wrong people and for the wrong reasons. Plus, the failure of interventions in Rwanda, Chechnya, and elsewhere made difficult conflicts worse than they should have been. It is clear that the international community has a lot to learn about how to conduct interventions effectively.

- Most legal scholars agree that pre-emptive war is no different from aggression in international law. Aggression is the supreme crime in international law. Accepting one pre-emptive war would open the floodgates to all preventive wars, reducing the world to the law of the jungle. This creates an environment where war can easily be justified.

Nuclear Disarmament

The following activity is adapted from *The Economist* 'Intelligent Business' series.

Split the class into two groups, representing two countries.

Country A has a nuclear energy program and wants to develop uranium for peaceful purposes. Country A is poor.

Country B believes this is a front for making weapons to wipe out their allies in the region. Country B is rich.

The two communities have to negotiate an agreement whereby Country A agrees to disband their program in return for an incentive from country B. If the incentive is not suitable they will refuse.

Give both communities enough of time and assign a 'President' to lead. Make sure they begin formally with proper decorum. Emphasise the diplomacy, thoroughness in the negotiation style as well as the need to create a win-win.

Vocabulary Refresh

Pre-emptive War – started in order to gain the advantage of *initiative* and to harm the enemy at a moment of minimal protection.

The greater good – a concept associated with the philosophy of utilitarianism.

Aggressive neighbour – hostile, antagonistic, violent, possibly unpredictable, usually hard-line.

Swift action – speedy action.

Humanitarian disaster – a situation whereby large parts of a civilian population are harmed.

Morally bankrupt – to be in no position to talk about moral issues because of the lack of morals one has demonstrated in the past.

Pragmatic – dealing with practical matters rather than theory, principles, or dogma.

Ideology – a set of views and theories that underpin a belief system.

Principles – rules, often that on which a prince should rule by.

Vicious – nasty, cruel, brutal and ferocious.

Weak liberals – people who fail to see the bad side of things.

Dictate – to rule with complete power.

Apathy – not caring about an important issue, simply through laziness.

A *tu quoque* argument – literally a 'you too argument', i.e. if you do something why can't I? This is a logical fallacy. See Class 23 – *Balancing the Budget*.

Cowardly – Lacking in courage. Poltroonery.

Democratic – Rule by the people.

International bullying – A strong country squeezing a weak country.

Unilateralist – Acting one one's own, without consent or advice from other countries in the international community.

Anarchy – lack of government, chaotic freedom.

The rule of law – principles in place, applicable to everyone, to control the population and provide justice, designed to prevent anarchy and promote fair civilized society.

Hindsight – being able to see something in retrospect; after the fact.

Hypocrites – people who preach one thing but do the opposite.

To open the floodgates – to allow completely something one had prohibited against.

The law of the jungle – survival of the strongest, lack of order and fairness.

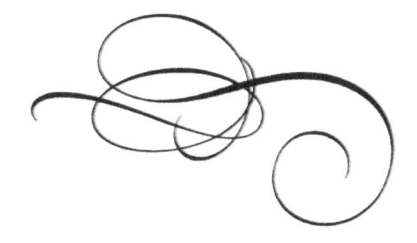

Debate 21 – Free Market

Debate 21 – Free Market

Is it a pity that many fortunes are made by people who just manipulate money and contribute nothing to society?

Goals of the Lesson

- For students to become more familiar with the concepts and ethical basis of taxation.
- For students to practice debating, using persuasive devices and functional phrases.
- For students to find some form of consensus on the issue.

Rhetoric

Discuss and demonstrate these figures of speech with the class and explain that people who are able to speak forcefully and persuasively often use devices like this. Tell the students that you would like them to try and use these devices during the debate.

1. **Metalepsis** – referring to something through reference to another thing to which it is remotely related. A type of **allusion** and **catachresis**.

'I've got to go catch the worm tomorrow.'

2. **Metaphor** – an implied comparison of two unlike things.

'Life's but a walking shadow; a poor player,
That struts and frets his hour upon the stage.'
~ Shakespeare, *The Tragedy of Macbeth*

3. **Metonymy** – substitution of a word to suggest what is really meant.

'The pen is mightier than the sword' – the words *pen* and *sword* signifying discourse and violence respectively.

'No. 10' as a synonym for the UK government.

Logical Fallacies

The Logical Fallacy is a rhetorical device which has no grounding in actual fact and is used by people to unfairly gain the upper hand in debates. Being able to spot such a flaw goes a long way to invalidating an opponent's argument.

1. **Tying the Question** – loading a fair question with an unfair, unrelated presupposition to make it seem they are one and the same. A type of trick question. See also **argument by question**.

'Do you favor the United States Army abolishing the affirmative-action program that produced Colin Powell? Yes or no?' ~ Bill Clinton

'Do you support freedom and the right to bear arms?' ~ Don Lindsay, *A List of Fallacious Arguments*

2. **Reifying** – aka the **pathetic fallacy** – the personification of a non-living thing to give it living qualities or giving an abstract thing concrete properties. Similar to **bad analogy**. A perfectly normal literary technique – see **anthropomorphism**.

'Nature abhors a vacuum.' ~ John Ruskin

'Religion attempts to destroy our liberty and is therefore immoral.'

'The universe will not allow the human race to die out by accident.'

3. **Slippery Slope Fallacy** – the assertion that something is wrong because it could slide towards something that is wrong.

'If we legalize soft drugs, then people will progress on to hard drugs.'

'If I make an exception for you, then I'll have to make an exception for everyone.'

Preamble

Some of this information is found on dozens of websites.

Beating the system as opposed to cheating the system (aka fraud). Is it acceptable? Do the ends justify the means, or do the means justify the ends? Is looking for shortcuts to wealth and success a misguided and foolhardy pursuit or is it our right? Discuss this quote: *If something seems too good to be true, then it probably is.* However some people are lucky, they happen to know the right people, or they are clever enough to skip school and still get good grades, etc etc.

Speculation – not to be confused with investment, although some speculation is necessary in investment.

George Soros, financier and philanthropist as well as an archetype of the 'post-capitalist' speculator and prophet, is flattered and feared at the same time. He is responsible for stock market crashes in some fifty countries. According to estimates, his fortune accounts for around 11 billion dollars. He financed campaigns aimed at preventing George W. Bush's re-election, in spite of the fact that he himself saved him from bankruptcy and is still working with his father in the Carlyle Group, a powerful financial organization. He has been active in many changes of governments and has been labeled a CIA cover. Soros first traded currencies during the Hungarian hyperinflation of 1945–1946. Soros emigrated to England in 1947 and moved to New York City in 1956, where he worked as a trader. He has stated that his intent was to earn enough money on Wall Street to support himself as an author and philosopher. On Black Wednesday (September 16, 1992), Soros became immediately famous when his fund sold short more than $10 billion worth of pounds. The Bank of England had to withdraw the currency from the European ERM and devalue the pound. Soros earned $ 1.1 billion in the process. He was dubbed 'the man who broke the Bank of England.' In 1997, during the Asian financial crisis, the Malaysian PM accused Soros of using his wealth to punish ASEAN for welcoming Burma as a member. He has given away more than $6 billion in philanthropic projects.

Despite working as an investor and currency speculator, he argues that the current system of financial speculation undermines healthy economic development in many underdeveloped countries. Soros blames many of the world's problems on the failures inherent in what he characterizes as market fundamentalism. His opposition to many aspects of globalization has made him a controversial figure. Victor Niederhoffer said of Soros: "Most of all, George believed even then in a mixed economy, one with a strong central international government to correct for the excesses of self-interest."

Soros claims to draw a distinction between being a participant in the market and working to change the rules that market participants must follow. According to Mahathir bin Mohamed, Prime Minister of Malaysia from 1981 to 2003, Soros – as the hedge fund chief of *Quantum* – may have been partially responsible for the 1997 East Asian crash when the Thai currency relinquished its peg to the dollar. According to Mahathir, in the three years leading to the crash, Soros was involved in short-term speculative investment in East Asian stock markets and real estate, then divested with 'indecent haste' at the first signs of currency devaluation. Soros replied, saying that Mahathir was using him "as a scapegoat for his own mistakes", that Mahathir's promises to ban currency trading (which Malaysian finance officials hastily retracted) were "a recipe for disaster" and that Mahathir "is a menace to his own country".

Market manipulation describes a deliberate attempt to interfere with the free and fair operation of the market and create artificial, false or misleading appearances with respect to the price of, or market for, a security, commodity or currency. Market manipulation can occur in multiple ways:

- Pools – agreements among a group of traders to delegate authority to a single manager to trade in a specific stock for a specific period of time and then to share in the resulting profits or losses
- Churning – when a trader places both buy and sell orders at about the same price. The increase in activity is intended to attract additional investors, and increase the price.
- Runs – when a group of traders create activity or rumors to drive the price of a security up.
- Ramping (the market) – actions designed to artificially raise the market price of listed securities and to give the impression of voluminous trading, in order to make a quick profit.
- Wash trade – selling and repurchasing the same or substantially the same security for the purpose of generating activity and increasing the price.
- Bear raid – attempting to push the price of a stock down by heavy selling or short selling.

Insider Trading – is trading a company's stock by people with access to non-public information about the company obtained or in breach of duty, trust and confidence. Anyone who misappropriates (steals) information from their employer and trades on that information in any stock (not just the employer's stock) is guilty of insider trading. There can be a grey area as to what constitutes insider trading.

Social Responsibility – is an ethical or ideological theory that an entity whether it is a government, corporation, organization or individual has a responsibility to society.

Social investors use four basic strategies to maximize financial return and attempt to maximize social good.

- Screening – excluding certain securities from investment consideration based on social and/or environmental criteria. For example, socially responsible investors may screen out tobacco company investments.
- Divesting – the act of removing stocks from a portfolio based on mainly ethical, non-financial objections to certain business activities of a corporation.
- Shareholder activism – efforts to positively influence corporate behavior. This includes initiating conversations with corporate management on issues of concern, and submitting and voting proxy resolutions. This undertaken with the belief that social investors can steer management on a course that will improve financial performance over time and enhance the well being of the stakeholders
- Positive investing – making investments in activities and companies believed to have a high and positive social impact.

Debating Phrases

<u>Challenges</u> – from Prime Minister's Questions

- Let's look at the judgments you have made.
- Isn't it clear that ….
- I've just said before that ….
- So I hope you'll agree that ….
- I think that you'll see ….
- As far as this is concerned, I'm aware that ….

The South-Sea Bubble – Edward Matthew Ward (1846)

The origins of the London Stock Exchange derive from this period when stockjobbers – a disreputable band of brokers based in local coffee houses – fleeced a gullible public of their savings based on promises of unlimited riches in non-existent South American business ventures. The frenzy of speculation swept the whole country and peaked in August 1720. This also coincided with the pricking of similar bubbles in France and Holland. The story forms the centerpiece of Charles' McKay's *Extraordinary Popular Delusions and the Madness of Crowds*.

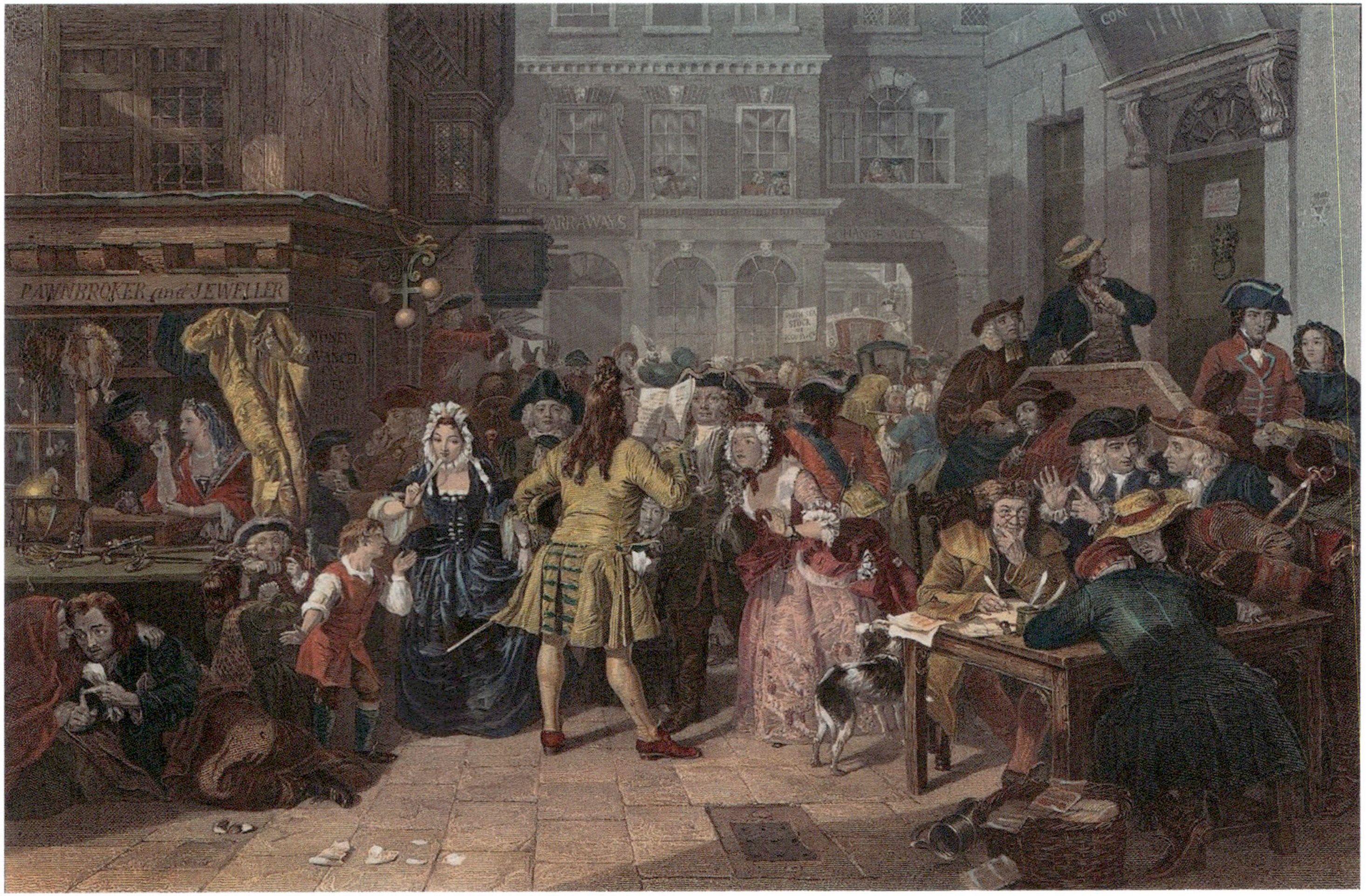
PAWNBROKER and JEWELLER

Yes, it is wrong that some people just manipulate money and give nothing to society.

- Some people are born into money, which is inherently unfair. Rich dynasties are not good for a country. They can grow to become more powerful than the government. It's the government's job to tax these individuals and redistribute the wealth to less advantaged people. This is how we create a better, more prosperous society in the long term; by giving everyone a level playing field.

- Capitalists have a responsibility to provide jobs. Without this they are just parasites on humanity. It is disgusting that people can live a superior lifestyle by simply shifting money from one place to another. It's not productive and not welcome here.

- These people don't produce anything and probably hide their money from the tax man. They are cheaters in every sense; always looking for the loopholes, always trying to be dishonest and hide their ill-gotten gains. I have no time for these people because they have no time for anyone but themselves and their own pockets.

- These people ought to learn the value of a hard day's work. They see what they do as a way to keep themselves in yachts and mansions. They don't really understand the value of money. Hard work makes an honest man. These people are not honest.

- These people should be heavily taxed to make their gains unprofitable. It's a very simple solution that would make money for the government and create a more homogenous and egalitarian society. The Europeans understand this, and the rest of the world needs to catch up and regulate against abuse of the system.

- The world would be a better place if every successful person was successful because they had contributed something – because they had used their skills and resources on the open market, not because they've used trickery and guile.

- We don't want a country where the rich get richer and the poor get poorer. Speculators make money because they have some secret, inside knowledge of how the markets work. They are dangerous and have power over governments and people's jobs. Let's put a stop to these manipulators and give the money to the needy.

- What message does cheating the system send to the rest of society? Don't work; look for the shortcuts in life. Just gamble and speculate. The sorry truth is that only 0.01percent of people can successfully do this. The rest get hurt and lose everything.

- This country was not founded by speculators. It was founded by honest, hard-working folk who gave all that they had. Don't let greedy fat cats steal it all away from us now. They have done nothing to deserve their huge salaries and bonuses. Society functions because of low paid workers like nurses and miners who give us care and electricity. The measure of good society is not how easy it is to become rich; it is about how well we take care of our weak.

It is not wrong.

- It's jealousy. People who complain about this are just envious that they were not quick or smart enough to do it themselves. Don't hurt the successful as a way to make up for your own shortcomings. It stifles healthy society and promotes mediocrity. We have seen from history what the politics of envy achieves: misery for all.

- It's a free country – why should individuals be obliged to "contribute" if they can find a legal way not to? We are not living in Nazi Germany. Freedom is the only way. Governments and do-gooders should stop interfering in people's private business dealings. It's not right or fair.

- There is a *very* high risk in shifting money around all the time. We often don't hear the stories of the people who lose everything. If you are willing to take the risk, surely you should be allowed to keep your reward, right?

- Whatever works for them – live and let live. Fortunately most speculators can do that and still be good people. Allowing a small amount of speculators gives everyone something to aspire to and a positive approach to life in general. We can win if we think smart. Life is not about drudgery and hard work; it's about seizing your chances.

- If you don't allow people to beat the system, you have no system. Limiting freedom to speculate means that you are undermining the free market which is fundamental to our society and without which everything else breaks down. Speculators are a lesser evil than the alternative – no opportunity for speculation.

- The wealth earned by the speculator is going to be spent on goods and services *somewhere*. His family is a likely beneficiary. The businesses he frequents (as well as new ones he'll want to try out) will benefit. Demand at the top end of society trickles down to everyone else. This is basic economics.

- It's not as regrettable as if they actually hurt society with their manipulations of money. Speculators are harmless people really. Why do we care what others do with their money? It's their money to start with. If they make more of it, well done I say.

- They should be given a pat on the back for being an individualist, risk-taking maverick. In a competitive world the smartest succeed. How can we have it any other way? The smartest aren't allowed the opportunity to succeed? We need these people because they show us the weaknesses of our system. People should not be punished for having courage and brains and using them. This is the system we choose.

- The freer a society is, the more prosperous it is. This is a law of laissez fair liberalism – which has proven success since the 19th century, most notably in Hong Kong. Therefore if something makes money, it must be good. Life is hard enough without being knocked for making a buck where you see opportunity.

Stock-Picking

Buy a copy of a newspaper with the stock market listings in it. Give a copy to each student and explain that the ideal portfolio for stock market investors should have around 12 companies in it (certainly no more than 20). This is because you don't want to put all your eggs in one basket but at the same time, if you pick a good company you want it to have a noticeable effect on your portfolio.

Tell the students they each have $10,000 to invest in one company. Ask each student to research and pick a stock from the listings based on their own research, opinions or intuitions. In other words, a firm which is a good business, has good products, good management, good marketing, good potential for the future, a suitable P/E ratio etc. Over the following few weeks you can check back to see who has made the biggest impact on the class portfolio.

Vocabulary

Inherently – intrinsically, naturally, essentially.

Parasites – an organism that lives off another. Parasites increase their fitness by exploiting hosts for food, habitat and dispersal while reducing the fitness of the host.

Loopholes – a weakness or exception that allows a system, such as a law or security, to be circumvented / avoided. They are searched for & used in elections, politics, criminal justice & security.

Their ill-gotten gains – obtained illegally or by improper means; dirty money.

Homogenous and egalitarian – all the same and fair.

Trickery and guile – deceit and cunning.

Shortcomings – failings.

Stifle – restrict.

Mediocrity – weakness, under-achieving.

Obliged – to be bound or forced to do something.

Do-gooders – people who interfere to try to right what they see as wrongs.

Aspire to something – to wish for something.

Drudgery – mundane, soul-destroying work.

Undermine – to destabilize, weaken, damage or chip away at someone's authority.

Maverick – an individualist who doesn't conform to normal rules, takes risks and rebels.

Making a buck – making a living, often a meager amount or conversely the result of a one off deal.

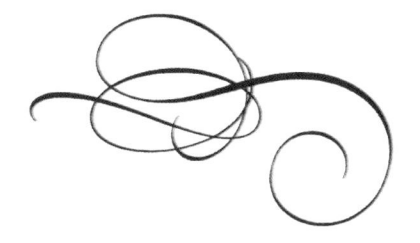

Debate 22 – Private Healthcare

Debate 22 – Private Healthcare

Those with the ability to pay should have the right to higher standards of medical care. Is this a good idea?

Goals of the Lesson

- For students to become more familiar with the concepts and ethical basis of taxation.
- For students to practice debating, using persuasive devices and functional phrases.
- For students to find some form of consensus on the issue.

Rhetoric

Discuss and demonstrate these figures of speech with the class and explain that people who are able to speak forcefully and persuasively often use devices like this. Tell the students that you would like them to try and use these devices during the debate.

1. **Neologism** – the use of a word or term that has recently been created, or has been in use for a short time. Opposite of **archaism**.

'Chindia' – a portmanteau coined by the Indian economist Jairam Ranesh.

2. **Onomatopoeia** – a word imitating a real sound e.g. 'tick-tock' or 'boom'.

'He has done his worst but the wound will end him.
He is hasped and hooped and hirpling with pain,
limping and looped in it.'
~ Seamus Heaney, *Beowulf*

3. **Oxymoron** – using two terms together, that normally contradict each other. Similar to **Irish bull**.

'Pretty ugly.'

Logical Fallacies

1. **Stacking the Deck** – or **special pleading** – a double standard where you allow the arguments that suit your position but not those against your position. Similar to **selective observation**.

'I'm not relying on faith in small probabilities here. These are slot machines, not roulette wheels. They are different.'

2. **Statement of Conversion** – in effect saying that your opponent still has a lot to learn. A patronizing **appeal to authority** of the speaker.

'I used to be just like you. I believed in evolution too but then I saw the light.'

3. **Stolen Concept** – **self-refuting idea** – a type of **internal contradiction** and **solipsism**. Using what you are trying to disprove. See also **begging the question**.

'All property is theft.' ~ Pierre-Joseph Proudhon. *Theft* as a concept depends on the existence of rightfully owned property in the first place.

'I am a liar, everything I say is a lie.'

'Physics has proven that science is incapable of showing us that anything is true.'

Preamble

The latter part of this taken from Wikipedia.

This debate is all the about the right to choose the best quality vs. the right to entitlement of the best. The argument becomes tricky because we are talking about a unique product in human society; healthcare – a matter of life and death, not just of individuals but of a whole nation. Therefore the root of this problem needs to address the benefits and shortcomings (failures) of the market system in the context of people's health and wealth or lack of it.

Important questions to consider:

1. Should the healthcare industry should be subject to the benefits / failures of the market?
2. Are the healthcare needs of a population beyond the capacity of a normal consumer market? In what degree is this so?
3. How big is the difference between the very best healthcare treatment and the bare minimum level of treatment provided by the state? How significant is this difference to the overall wellbeing of the majority?
4. Do we really want an equal system paid for by the rich through taxation? Is this a waste of money and resources? Could this harm the economy of a nation?
5. Should we deny people a service that doesn't break any laws if they are willing and able to pay for it? Where do you draw the line? No Häagen Dazs ice cream in bed? No silk sheets for those who want them? Is this fair?
6. Is it fundamentally immoral to have a two tier society where one small group can afford while others go without?
7. Is the health of nation a major concern to a government?
8. Is an unfettered private sector following the profit motive a healthy thing, encouraging increased wealth in society and spurring innovation?
9. Which other industries are supposed to be beyond the rule of market forces? Defence, education, lighthouses and other public goods.
10. Why should the presence of a public good preclude it from being owned and profitable in some way, under a different guise or targeted to a certain group?
11. What does a totally egalitarian system say about a country? What does it say about the way people are expected to see and treat each other and what does it say about the way in which the government values its responsibility? What values are worth doing this for?

Consider this: *The inherent vice of capitalism is the unequal sharing of blessings; the inherent virtue of socialism is the equal sharing of miseries.* ~ Winston Churchill

Public goods

If a good is a public good, no one can be excluded from using it and secondly if one person uses it, that does not diminish the amount available for consumption by another party. But the question is, is healthcare really a public good when hospitals are overcrowded and doctors and medicines are in short supply and buildings and standards are generally crumbling under the strain of constant use?

Market Failures

Market failures can be viewed as scenarios where individuals' pursuit of pure self-interest leads to results that are not efficient – that can be improved upon from the societal point-of-view. Market failures are often associated with non-competitive markets or public goods. The existence of a market failure is often used as a justification for government intervention. However, some types of government interventions, such as taxes, subsidies, bailouts, wage and price controls, and regulations, may also lead to an inefficient allocation of resources, (sometimes called government failures). Thus, there is often a choice between imperfect outcomes, i.e. imperfect market outcomes with or without government interventions.

Market failure can occur in 2 main ways which ultimately come down to the imperfect control of property rights:

First, the actions of a seller can cause external problems. For example, a steel maker absorbs labor, capital and other inputs and these costs will be reflected in the market price for steel. If the firm also pollutes the atmosphere and if it is not forced to pay for this, then this cost will be borne by society. In this case, the market equilibrium in the steel industry will not be optimal. More steel will be produced than would occur were the firm to have to pay for all of its costs of production. This would be a failure for the 'yes' camp's reasoning. I.e. the poor are excluded and deprived of good healthcare by price barriers, fostering inequality in society.

Second, a seller can gain market power, allowing them to block other beneficial trade occurring. This can lead to inefficiency due to imperfect competition, which can take many different forms, such as monopolies and cartels. These will use their market power to restrict output and competition so as to keep prices and profits high. This would be a failure of the 'no' camp's argument. I.e. the state forms a monopoly in healthcare thus excluding choice & stifling quality for society.

Debating Phrases

<u>Asking / giving clarification</u> – from Prime Minister's Questions

- Why is that …?
- Will it be likely that …?
- It is evident that …?
- And therefore I say specifically that ….
- We can safely predict that ….?
- Will you agree with me that …?

Plague Hospital – Francisco de Goya (1800)

This painting is from Saragossa during the Peninsula War, which was fought to expel Napoleon from Spain. The British could only pay for the war because Nathan Rothschild had gold smuggled to Wellington in Portugal. The nation was war-torn and impoverished and the Plague was rife in the many military hospitals at the time. The wretched patients are doomed to death in a darkened squalid cellar, excluded from all others. The sun shines through the window symbolizing a new world that awaits them after death.

Great Debates

Yes, those who can pay should have the right to higher standards of medical care.

- Medical care is no more of a right than food is a right. If someone can provide excellent medical care at a price, then we should have the right to buy that care. Having the right to *transact* with someone is not the same as a right to *have* it. Excellent medical care is expensive and scarce – not everybody can have it. Let those who can, pay for it and make sure that everybody else gets care that is good enough.

- Sometimes treatments cost too much money and would bankrupt everyone except the wealthiest people. But if Tom Cruise wants an ultrasound machine he should be able to have one. Public hospitals are in such a bad way that many refuse to use them and travel overseas for care. Many people don't want these appalling conditions so it is their right to use their own money to find better treatment.

- Private healthcare can help to support public healthcare and inject money into the system. It is like a goose that lays golden eggs. The government should control the private sector and make a profit from it. That way everyone is a winner. Let the rich have their luxury service but let the rest of us benefit from that. Bad health and death are facts of life. Why should there not be a profit in them?

- There is almost no limit to how much can be spent to keep someone alive. But the government can't afford to say 'the sky's the limit' to everyone with health problems. So, the government also cannot say 'you are not allowed to buy extra medical treatment that will save your life' to those who *can* pay for it.

- Someone in my street has a Rolls Royce does not mean the govt should pay for everyone to have this. It would bankrupt the nation. Public healthcare is not free – nothing is truly free in this world expect the air you breathe. Healthcare costs money. Even though it is a public good, someone has to pay for it. Having a private system reduces the burden on taxpayer, so it can be better and more affordable for the rest.

Great Debates

- We don't live in an ideal world. It would be nice if everyone could afford luxury service but surely adequate service will do. There is a minimum standard to stay alive and recover and that is the only responsibility the government needs to worry about.

- Why should the government take care of everything and everyone? Rich people worked hard to make their money and they should spend it as they wish. Why should the government look after everyone and spend **our** money doing that? This country is strongest when people can stand on their own two feet. If you can't pay for it, you don't deserve it. This is how the world works in every other market…

- New machines and medicines need a private sector to discover them, and then they can be made more affordable to everybody else. The private system drives forward research in the industry through the 'profit motive' so in the long term everyone can benefit. Private healthcare is a good thing and it saves the taxpayer a lot of money.

No, rich people should not have the right to higher medical care.

- It creates a privileged elite. If one excellent standard is available, why should everyone be deprived? Two tier systems are unfair. They are not egalitarian and do not foster solidarity. The poorest people receive a lower standard of healthcare. That means poor people will continue to get sicker and rich people will continue to get healthier, increasing the gap between rich and poor.

- Is the life of a rich person is worth more than the life of a poor person? In a modern society this kind of inequality is a disgrace. This is not what our forefathers fought for. It's like the wealthy live in a different country with different rules. Medical care should not be about how much you can pay. One person's health and life is not worth more than another's because he can pay more.

- Rich people have been abusing poor people for hundreds of years, yet they live longer and get better medical care? This could not be more unfair. It's about time the government leveled the playing field and made the rich pay for better hospitals through taxation – they can easily afford it.

- Why should the government stand back when they have the ability to improve healthcare standards for everyone? In a truly fair society, healthcare is the responsibility of the state and the very highest standards should be free for all. This is not too much to ask for in a modern society. The less the poor need to worry about healthcare the more productive our country can be and the more pride and confidence people will have.

- Healthcare is a basic human right. If we separate healthcare into two groups then new medicines and innovations are kept secret and not made available when they should be and could be. This slows down our economy and makes our country weak. If the elite get good treatment, they just get stronger and stronger while the people who really need healthcare can't get it. Someone needs to redress the balance.

- The poor need an advantage in life, not to be treated as third-class citizens. The rich are greedy and never help anyone, unless they are forced too. We need to value our fellow citizens more, just like a big family. You would not let your family suffer just because they have no money. Having a two tier system sends the wrong message, that the government doesn't care about its people and we live in a selfish society.

- Scandinavia and Canada have the fairest and wealthiest societies in the world and their healthcare system is wholly government funded (private health insurance is illegal in Quebec). If we had private sector-standard healthcare for all, we would live in an even better society. People don't want choice if everything they need is provided for them. This causes less stress and this is really the government's job.

- Inequality is the worst thing for society as a whole because it causes revolutions, crime and war. If our people are not respected, we will rise up and take what is theirs.

Cosmetic Surgery

Explain that in the UK, and presumably other European countries, you can have a sex change paid for by the National Health Service. See whether the students think this is a good idea or not.

Ask the students which one feature they would personally like to change with cosmetic surgery. Then have the students look up local clinics which provide such feature enhancing surgery to ask for detailed information and inquire about prices. Each student must try to get as much information as they can without committing to an appointment. After the phone calls have been completed, get everyone to relate their findings to the class.

Vocabulary

Transact – to do business, hand over money.

Scarce – rare, hard to find.

Bankrupt – insolvent, unable to pay debts.

Ultrasound machine – a machine for scanning fetuses in the womb.

Inject money – to force (a fluid) into a passage, cavity, or tissue or more appropriately in this context, to introduce money into a decrepid organization or system.

The sky's the limit – there is no limit. Infinite potential.

Adequate – satisfactory.

Profit motive – an invisible force that gets people out of bed in the morning.

Rolls Royce – a motor vehicle driven by wealthy people / those who like to display their wealth.

The burden on taxpayer – the amount of hard earned cash the weary tax payer has to shell out.

Privileged elite – and handful of people born with a silver spoon in their mouths.

Deprived – unable to access basic goods and services.

Egalitarian – someone who believes that all humans should have equal rights and opportunities.

Solidarity – the intense bond between members of a (usually downtrodden) political group.

Innovation – creating something brilliant in such a way that it takes twice as long and costs three times as much as the old fashioned way of doing the same thing.

Redress the balance – to set things straight.

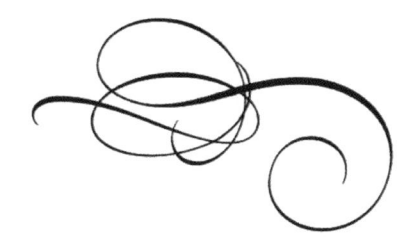

Debate 23 – Balancing the Budget

Great Debates

Debate 23 – Balancing the Budget

Should taxpayers be expected to prop up any theatres or museums that cannot survive on a commercial basis?

Goals of the Lesson

- For students to become more familiar with the concepts and ethical basis of taxation.
- For students to practice debating, using persuasive devices and functional phrases.
- For students to find some form of consensus on the issue.

Rhetoric

Discuss and demonstrate these figures of speech with the class and explain that people who are able to speak forcefully and persuasively often use devices like this. Tell the students that you would like them to try and use these devices during the debate.

1. **Parable** – an extended **metaphor** told as an anecdote to illustrate or teach a moral lesson.

   A water bearer in China had two large pots, each hung on the ends of a pole which he carried across his neck. One of the pots had a crack in it, while the other pot was perfect and always delivered a full portion of water. At the end of the long walk from the stream to the house, the cracked pot arrived only half full. For a full two years this went on daily, with the bearer delivering only one and a half pots full of water to his house. Of course, the perfect pot was proud of its accomplishments, perfect for which it was made. But the poor cracked pot was ashamed of its own imperfection, and miserable that it was able to accomplish only half of what it had been made to do. After 2 years of what it perceived to be a bitter failure, it spoke to the water bearer one day by the stream. "I am ashamed of myself because this crack in my side causes water to leak all the way back to your house."

   The bearer said to the pot, "Did you notice that there were flowers only on your side of the path, but not on the other pot's side? That's because I have always known about your flaw, and I planted flower seeds on your side of the path, and every day while we walk back, you've watered them. For two years I have been able to pick these beautiful flowers to decorate the table. Without you being just the way you are, there would not be this beauty to grace the house."

Moral: Each of us has our own unique flaws. We're all crackpots. But it's the cracks and flaws we each have that make our lives together so very interesting and rewarding. You've just got to take each person for what they are, and look for the good in them.

2. **Paradiastole** – deliberate redescription of something to show it in a positive or negative light. Similar to **euphemism**.

E.g. calling a vain person 'confident' or calling a miserly person 'frugal'.

3. **Paradox** – use of apparently contradictory ideas to point out some underlying truth. See stolen concept in the previous lesson's logic section.

'I can resist anything except temptation.' ~ Oscar Wilde

Logical Fallacies

The Logical Fallacy is a rhetorical device which has no grounding in actual fact and is used by people to unfairly gain the upper hand in debates. Being able to spot such a flaw goes a long way to invalidating an opponent's argument.

1. **Straw Man** – arguing against something which is not really a valid concern. Sometimes in order to win a fight you need to create an enemy, if you don't already have one.

Dave   Nude bathing is healthy and nude beaches should be permitted here.
Bill   No. That kind of free sex threatens the morality of society.

'Senator Jones says that we should not fund the attack submarine program. I disagree entirely. I can't understand why he wants to leave us defenceless like that.' ~ from Nizkor.org

The US and UK's determination to prosecute Saddam Hussein for the possession of 'weapons of mass destruction' prior to the 2003 invasion of Iraq.

2. **Tu Quoque** – the 'You Too' argument – or 'two wrongs make a right'. The arguer charges his enemies with hypocrisy when his enemies' behaviour is actually irrelevant to the veracity of the point at hand. A type of **ad hominem**.

'The West has no right condemn Russia's invasion of Georgia. Just look at what they have done in Afghanistan.'

3. **Weasel Wording** – similar to **euphemism** but more formal and deceitful. Also includes manipulative grammar e.g. hedging and vagueness.

'An American President may not legally conduct a war without a declaration of Congress. So, various Presidents have conducted 'police actions', 'armed incursions', 'protective reaction strikes', 'pacification', 'safeguarding American interests', and a wide variety of 'operations'.' ~ Carl Sagan, *The Fine Art of Baloney Detection*

'An important art of politicians is to find new names for institutions which under old names have become odious to the public.' ~ Talleyrand, infamous French diplomat

The many examples of newspeak in George Orwell's *1984*.

Preamble

Partly adapted from Wikipedia.

Questions to Consider

Are cultural institutions considered public goods? That is, should they be made available to such an extent that people can appreciate (consume) as much as they wish and the cost of this be borne by the taxpayer? Why are theatres public goods? Because the tickets are usually too expensive for commoners but their product is valuable to all of society? The question is, are they a *necessity* to all of society? What is the role of art in our society and how much should it be valued? More or less than it is now? Who decides? Is it fair to exclude people from enjoying the fine arts and high culture? Maybe poor people don't place a high importance on these goods? Should this change? Who is to say?

Public Spiritedness

Public mindedness may be encouraged by non-market solutions to economic problems, such as tradition and social norms. Public spiritedness of a limited type is the basis for voluntary contributions that support public radio, television and online collaborative media like Wikipedia. Groups relying on such social norms often have a federated structure, since collaboration emerges more readily in smaller social groups than in large ones. This is why labor unions or charities are often organized this way.

Philanthropy

Philanthropy derives from Ancient Greek, meaning 'to love people'. Philanthropy is the act of donating money, goods, services, time and/or effort to support a socially beneficial cause with a defined objective and with no financial or material reward to the donor. Philanthropy is a major source of income for fine arts and performing arts, religious, and humanitarian causes as well as educational institutions.

Who practices the support of unprofitable theatres and museums?

The French and the Europeans in general are famously good at this. Perhaps they are not as obsessed by money as the rest of us, but it is more likely that they hold culture in high esteem and do not put just a monetary value on it.

Debating Phrases

<u>Reasoning</u> – from Prime Minister's questions

- I wholeheartedly agree with you.
- The fact that is necessary to point out is that ….
- Of course I agree that ….
- Clearly this is a case of ….
- Our focus should be ….

Samson Slaying a Philistine – Giambologna (1562)

This classic Italian sculpture was made for the Medicis of Florence as a way of showing their cultural superiority over rival cities. The piece made its way via Spain, to England in 1623 and is now housed in the Victoria and Albert Museum. It was inspired by an earlier sculpture by Michelangelo.

The Philistines were a group of people in biblical times who were enemies of the Jews. This is where we get the modern name *Palestine*. The Philistines were depicted as barbarous and uncultured in comparison with other peoples of the region and thus to call a person a philistine is to imply that they are ignorant and uncouth. One big worry for intellectuals is the decline of modern society into philistinism due to economic pressures. Likewise, admiration and preservation of the arts is something the Victorians felt very strongly about.

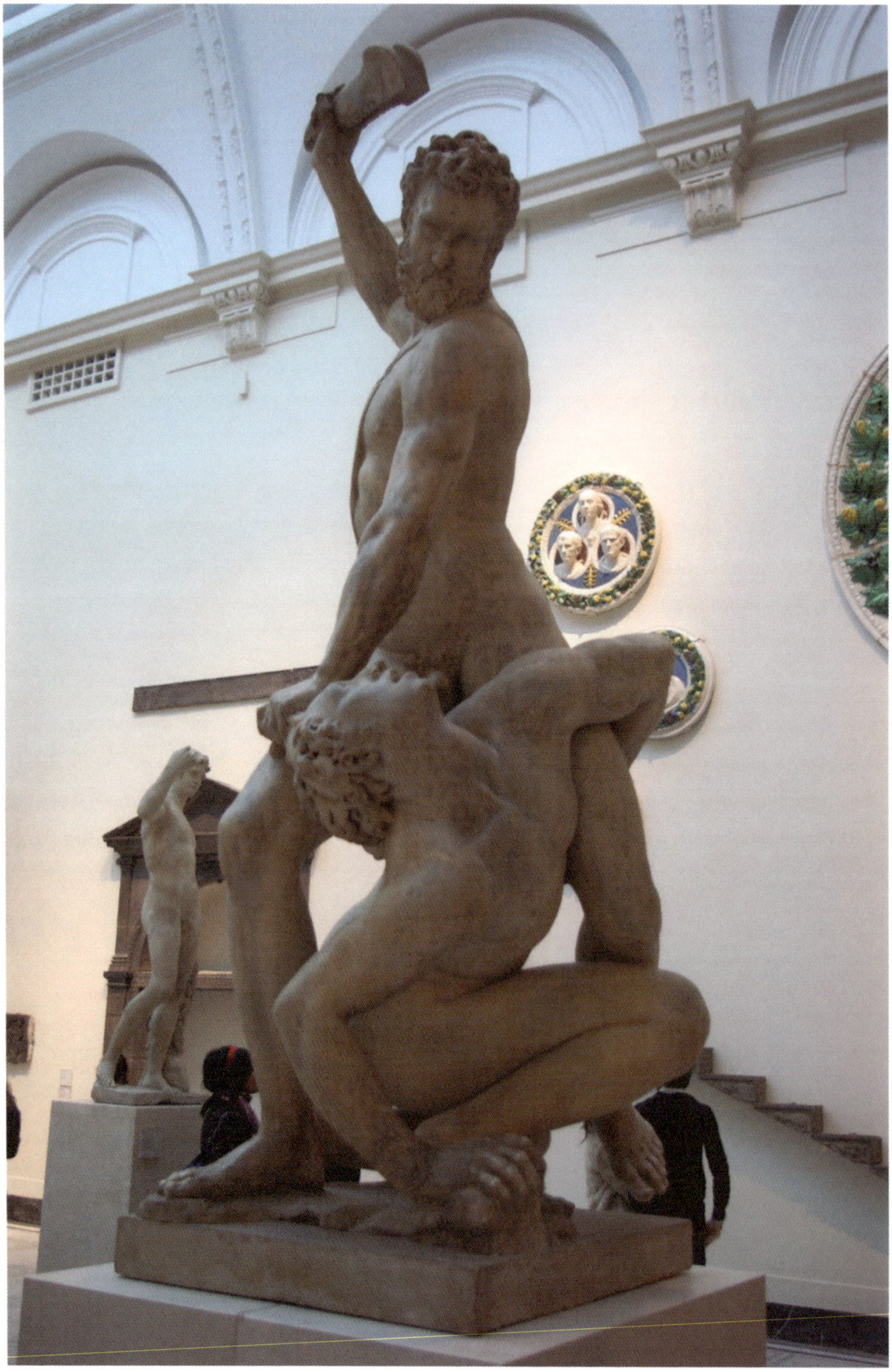

Great Debates

Yes, taxpayers should prop up some non-profitable institutions.

- Many things that are supported by the treasury aren't commercially viable. Of course some unprofitable theatres and museums aren't worth propping-up, but we should trust that such decisions can be made. The government knows what is best for us. We don't want to become a nation of philistines. That's regression, not progress.

- Art and culture should not have to be commercially successful to continue existing – the benefits we get from them are more important. Some things can't be measured on a balance sheet – some things are measured beyond money. To value things only in terms of money is for classless bean counters. Culture is divine. We need money to survive but we culture to live. Currently only rich people can benefit from culture.

- Just because something cannot survive on a commercial basis does not mean that it's not financially worth it. Some examples are public education, social security, the police force, roads & street lights, the Food and Drug Administration, Fire & Rescue, parks and libraries. I believe that theatres and museums in particular are things that need to be placed in this category. Poor people need access to these things.

- This is a problem of our society's lack of cultural awareness. We are all too concerned about making money and working in boring offices pushing paperwork around that we have no time or desire to appreciate the beautiful things in life. This is a sad reflection on how little people care for culture. The government needs to educate people more and the media has a responsibility to do that so that failing museums, theatres and art galleries can make more revenue.

- I think that art is something that needs to be sponsored. It's hard to make a living on art, but art greatly improves human progress. This progress is real human progress, not technological progress. Art expands our perspectives. Museums expand knowledge; similar to what the public education system does. Art cultivates our soul.

- All museums in London are free. This is socialist and good. The government has a responsibility to support as much art as it can. The government must actively invest in public art projects. It greatly improves our wellbeing. If more people are free to work in cultural organizations, our economy will benefit. Creative people increase the GDP so the government should actively support these weak industries.

- We need to look at the root cause for failing cultural ventures. This is not about them being poor quality. This is about them being unheard of. The only people who can spend the marketing dollars to keep such things open are wealthy individuals or governments. Unfortunately wealthy donors are few and far between as rich people don't like to part with their money. The government has to step in.

- We ought to be more generous as a society. People who don't want to support valuable institutions are mean and greedy and have no class. Let's not have them in charge of public policy. Public sector projects must also reinvest their profits to improve their service too. Private sector enterprises do not always do this.

No, taxpayers should not prop up non-profitable organizations.

- This question is a false opposition: survive on a commercial basis vs. survive based on taxpayer money. Art can be privately funded in a non-commercial way. That means rich people can decide to fund any failing projects they like. The private sector therefore has the capacity to handle what needs to be handled and take up the slack.

- The market is the best judge. If something cannot survive in the market it is obviously not good enough to be worthy of artificial life support. Let the market decide. This is natural. Any worthy museum or art gallery should make a profit. Why would a good one not make a profit?

- Art does not make the world a better place. Food and shelter do. Shouldn't the government focus on more serious issues in our society than mere pretty objects and old clay pots in a museum? What is the world coming to? History is bunk and art is for wasters. People need to do something more worthwhile.

- Haven't we got enough needy causes to worry about as a society, than supporting some businesses which are probably in trouble because of bad management anyway? Looking at art and going to the theatre is nice but we can easily live without it.

- I will only give money to people or groups who can't help themselves like battered and abused kids or animal homes or old people's homes. Why should my tax money go on funding luxuriant art spaces and high salaries for public servants? It's not right. People who work in cultural institutions are over-paid and over-educated. Welcome to the real world everybody! There is risk in every money making venture so why is culture so different that it has to be risk free? I don't see government bailing out badly performing stores. If the reward for poor quality is government money then we are in serious trouble as a creative and productive economy.

- No wonder our economy is in so much trouble when the government makes unprofitable businesses a priority. Some things you can't fix just by throwing money at them. That money may as well be poured down the drain. Privatize the profits and nationalize the losses? I don't think so. Why does the public have to pick up the tab every time something goes wrong? This is a problem in our culture where cheating the taxpayer is seen as normal.

- The greatest art, theatre and so on came from the Renaissance and from the ancient world. They didn't have tax dollars to support them! Shakespeare didn't survive on tax payer handouts. Poorly performing theatres need complete management shakeups and they need to respond better to the market. The reason they are in trouble is because they are stuck in the past and they refuse to lower their prices.

- Let them go to the wall. Sink or swim baby. Do or die. In this world there are no free lunches. Art has to be worth something – if nobody will pay for it, it is not art and therefore it is junk. Nobody pays for junk. Our society is better off without junk.

Hosting the Olympics

Ask the students to write a letter to one of their national newspapers explaining why their city should put in a bid to hold the Olympic Games. Students have to argue how, despite the cost, the games would be worth it.

Some things to consider.

National image and pride.
Regional image and pride.
Tourist revenue.
Cultural impact.
Political impact.
Viable sources of funding.
Security issues.
Urban development.
Legacy.
Financial cost.
Business and marketing opportunities.

Vocab Refresh

The treasury – a place (or department) where the funds of the government, of a corporation, or the like are deposited, kept, and disbursed.

Commercially viable – to have a long-term future as a money-making going concern.

Propping-up – to support, or prevent from falling.

Philistine – an uncultured ignorant person who knows nothing about the arts. From the Bible, i.e. the people of ancient Palestine.

Balance sheet – a snapshot of a company's financial health.

Classless – lacking in refinement, social distinction and cultural awareness.

Bean counters – beans are a cheap commodity, so to count them is a rather silly thing to do. A 'bean counter' is one who nitpicks over small things in order to save costs. It is a derogatory term for accountants, bankers, and anyone who holds a financial interest in an endeavor.

Divine – better than perfect. What people will say if they read a book or eat something that is better than perfect.

Perspectives – viewpoints, ways of perceiving things.

Few and far between – not many, sparse.

Part with – to give away.

Take up the slack – to do the work which someone else has stopped doing, but which still needs to be done. *Nautical* – pick up the slack rope because someone else has dropped it.

History is bunk – quote by Henry Ford, meaning studying history is a meaningless waste of time.

Waster – a person of talent or intelligence who deliberately steers their course towards matters of a dubious nature. Somebody with the capacity for success who fails on purpose.

Go to the wall – to lose, be defeated, go bankrupt.

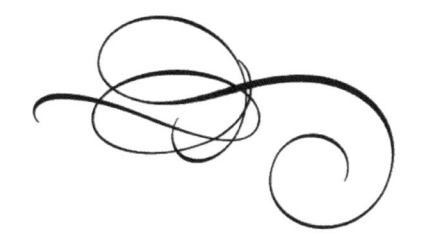

Debate 24 – Cultural Relativism

Debate 24 – Cultural Relativism

There are no savage and civilized peoples; only different cultures. Is this true?

Goals of the Lesson

- For students to become more familiar with the concepts and ethical basis of taxation.
- For students to practice debating, using persuasive devices and functional phrases.
- For students to find some form of consensus on the issue.

Rhetoric

Discuss and demonstrate these figures of speech with the class and explain that people who are able to speak forcefully and persuasively often use devices like this. Tell the students that you would like them to try and use these devices during the debate.

1. **Parallelism** – the use of similar structures in two or more clauses.

'The inherent vice of capitalism is the *unequal sharing* of blessing; the inherent virtue of socialism is the *equal sharing* of miseries.' ~ Winston Churchill

2. **Paraprosdokian** – unexpected ending or truncation of a clause.

'You can always count on Americans to do the right thing – after they've tried everything else.' ~ Winston Churchill

3. **Parenthesis** – insertion of a clause or sentence in a place where it interrupts the natural flow of the sentence.

'She concluded by throwing me – I often served as a connubial missile – at Joe, who, glad to get hold of me on any terms, passed me on into the chimney and quietly fenced me up there with his great leg.' ~ Charles Dickens, *Great Expectations*

Logical Fallacies

The Logical Fallacy is a rhetorical device which has no grounding in actual fact and is used by people to unfairly gain the upper hand in debates. Being able to spot such a flaw goes a long way to invalidating an opponent's argument.

1. **Wisdom of the Ancients** – the arguer must be right or more learned because he or she invokes an idea that has been around for a long time or resist change by praising what happened in the past. Conversely the arguer may praise very new ideas because of their fashionableness, or gush about what people do nowadays. Similar to **appeal to tradition** and **bandwagon jumping**.

Boris Johnson claimed in his book, *The Dream of Rome*, that the Romans ran Europe better than the EU. He failed to note that the population in ancient times was much smaller, was uneducated and immobile while the Romans were dictators and could do whatever they wanted.

2. **Contrarian Argument** – insincere or provocative disagreement for the sake of being different or getting attention or a reaction. See **trolling** on the internet.

'Amateurs are better than experts.' ~ James Surowiecki, *The Wisdom of Crowds*

'What's the giraffe's most distinctive feature? Hint: It's not the neck.' ~ *Slate Magazine*

3. **Affirming the Consequent** – logic reversal – a statement of the form 'if P then Q' gets turned into 'Q therefore P'. Oversimplifying and taking **occam's razor** to an extreme. See also **false cause**.

If I have the flu, then I have a sore throat.
I have a sore throat.
Therefore, I have the flu.

Preamble

The following information is taken from Wikipedia.

Cultural relativism is the idea that an individual human's beliefs and activities should be understood in terms of his or her own culture, not by analyzing them through the eyes of another, more dominant culture. This principle was established as self-evident in anthropological research by Franz Boas in the first few decades of the 20th century.

Boas believed we should examine the individual, not the group so as not to ignore one of Charles Darwin's main contributions to evolutionary theory – that in reality there are no distinct 'species' only differencing individuals and that classification is not an explanation.

Cultural relativism was in part a response to Western ethnocentrism. Ethnocentrism holds that there is universality to Western culture and this applies to all cultures. Every culture of the world is measured against a benchmark of Western civilization which is considered to be the most desirable of civilizations. Ethnocentrism may take obvious forms, in which one consciously believes that one's people's arts are the most beautiful, values the most virtuous, and beliefs the most truthful. Ethnocentrism is when one's own culture limits one's perceptions. It is the viewpoint that one's own group is the center of everything against which all other groups are judged. Cultural relativism on the other hand, calls attention to the importance of the local context in understanding the meaning of particular human beliefs and activities.

This poses 2 questions for cross-cultural communicators:

1. How to escape the unconscious bonds of one's own culture, which inevitably bias our perceptions of and reactions to the world?
2. How to make sense of an unfamiliar culture?

Moral Relativism means that there are no absolute or universal moral standards or truths. Therefore it is wrong to force the moral standards of one society on another. In other words, ethics differ from one culture to another depending on the social, cultural, personal and historical circumstances of that culture. There are no concrete absolute rights or wrongs.

Some moral relativists for example, Jean-Paul Sartre hold that a personal and subjective moral core lies or ought to lie at the base of individuals' moral acts. In this view public morality reflects social convention, and only personal, subjective morality expresses true authenticity – i.e. following one's conscience.

History records relativist positions over several thousand years. Protagoras' assertion (c. 481 – 420 BC) that "man is the measure of all things" might provide an early philosophical precursor to modern relativism, but it is not clear whether Protagoras has in mind moral relativism or something else. The Greek historian Herodotus (c. 484 – 420 BC) observed that each society regards its own belief system and way of doing things as better than all others. Various ancient philosophers also questioned the idea of an objective standard of morality.

David Hume (1711 – 1776) distinguished between matters of fact and matters of value, and suggested that moral judgments consist of the latter, for they do not deal with verifiable facts obtained in the world, but only with our sentiments and passions. But Hume regarded some of our sentiments as universal. He famously denied that morality has any objective standard, and suggested that the universe remains indifferent to our preferences and our troubles.

In the 20th century the increasing body of knowledge of great differences in belief among societies caused both social scientists and philosophers to question whether any objective, absolute standards pertaining to values could exist. This led some to posit that differing systems have equal validity, with no standard for adjudicating among conflicting beliefs. The Finnish philosopher-anthropologist Edward Westermarck (1862 – 1939) portrayed all moral ideas as subjective judgments that reflect one's upbringing. He rejected G.E. Moore's (1873 – 1958) ethical intuitionism – in vogue during the early part of the 20th century, and which identified moral propositions as true or false, and known to us through a special faculty of intuition – because of the obvious differences in beliefs among societies, which he said provided evidence of the lack of any innate, intuitive power.

Some evolutionary biologists believe that morality is a natural phenomenon that evolved by natural selection acting at the individual level, and through group selection. Consequently many view morality as being relative, constituting any set of social behaviours that promoted the survival and successful reproduction of humans.

Various historical and cultural events and practices (including the Holocaust, racism, Stalinism, apartheid in South Africa, genocide, unjust wars, genital mutilation, slavery, terrorism, Nazism, etc.) present difficult problems for relativists, because these acts, which are condemned by the "majority of people" everywhere, are not absolutely "bad" from a relativist perspective. This is, in fact, exactly what moral relativism states, and there is no self-contradiction in it.

Universal Morality is the position that some system of ethics applies for all individuals regardless of culture, race, sex, religion, nationality, sexuality, or other distinguishing feature. An enormous range of traditions and thinkers have supported one form or another of moral universalism, from the ancient Platonists and Stoics, through Christians and Muslims, to modern Kantian,

Objectivist, natural rights, human rights and utilitarian thinkers. The United Nations' Universal Declaration of Human Rights is an example of moral universalism in practice. Noam Chomsky states that

> 'In fact, one of the, maybe the most, elementary of moral principles is that of universality, that is, if something's right for me, it's right for you; if it's wrong for you, it's wrong for me. Any moral code that is even worth looking at has that at its core somehow.'

The source or justification of a universal ethic may be thought to be, for instance, human nature, shared vulnerability to suffering, the demands of universal reason, what is common among existing moral codes, or the common mandates of religion.

Binary opposition in post-structuralism is seen as one of several influential characteristics or tendencies of Western and Western-derived thought, and that typically, one of the two opposites assumes a role of dominance over the other. The categorization of binary oppositions is often value-laden and ethnocentric, with an illusory order and superficial meaning. The critique of binary oppositions is an important part of post-feminism, post-colonialism, post-anarchism, and critical race theory, which argue that the perceived binary dichotomy between man/woman, civilized/savage, and caucasian/non-caucasian have perpetuated and legitimized Western power structures favouring "civilized" white men.

Post-structural criticism of binary oppositions is not simply the reversal of the opposition, but its deconstruction, which is described as apolitical – that is, not intrinsically favouring one arm of a binary opposition over the other. Deconstruction is the "event" or "moment" at which a binary opposition is thought to contradict itself, and undermine its own authority. Although deconstruction can not explain how a rational basis for defending itself can then be maintained after it has removed any objective basis in structuralism it may have had.

Value judgments are judgments of the rightness or wrongness of something, or of the usefulness of something, based on a personal view. As a generalization, a value judgment can refer to a judgment based upon a particular set of values or on a particular value system. The term *value judgment* can be used both in a positive sense, signifying that a judgment must be made taking a value system into account, or in a disparaging sense, signifying a judgment made by personal whim rather than rational, objective thought.

In its positive sense, recommendation to make a value judgment is an admonition to consider carefully, to avoid whim and impetuousness, and search for consonance with one's deeper convictions. In its disparaging sense the term *value judgment* implies a conclusion is insular, one-sided, and not objective – contrasting with judgments based upon deliberation, balance and rationality.

Most commonly the term *value judgment* refers to an individual's opinion. Of course, the individual's opinion is formed to a degree by their belief system, and the culture to which they belong. So a natural extension of the term *value judgment* is to include declarations seen one way from one value system, but which may be seen differently from another. Conceptually this extension of definition is related both to the anthropological axiom "cultural relativism" (that is, that cultural meaning derives from a context) and to the term "moral relativism" (that is, that moral and ethical propositions are not universal truths, but stem from cultural context). In the pejorative sense, a value judgment formed within a specific value system may be parochial, and may be subject to dispute in a wider audience.

The White Man's Burden is a poem by the English poet Rudyard Kipling. Imperialists within the United States latched onto the phrase as a justification for imperialism as a noble enterprise. At face value it appears to be a command to white men to colonize and rule people of other nations for their own benefit (both the people and the duty may be seen as representing the 'burden' of the title). The phrase has become emblematic both of eurocentric racism and of Western aspirations to dominate the developing world.

A Eurocentric analysis of the poem may conclude that Kipling presents a eurocentric view of the world, in which non-European cultures are seen as childlike. This view proposes that white people consequently have an obligation to rule over, and encourage the cultural development of people from other ethnic and cultural backgrounds until they can take their place in the world by fully adopting Western ways. The term "the white man's burden" has been interpreted as racist, or taken as a metaphor for a condescending view of non-Western national culture and economic traditions, identified as a sense of European ascendancy which has been called "cultural imperialism". An alternative interpretation is the philanthropic view, common in Kipling's formative years, that the rich have a moral duty and obligation to help "the poor" "better" themselves whether the poor want the help or not.

The first step towards lightening

The White Man's Burden

is through teaching the virtues of cleanliness.

Pears' Soap

is a potent factor in brightening the dark corners of the earth as civilization advances, while amongst the cultured of all nations it holds the highest place—it is the ideal toilet soap.

Debating Phrases

Socratic Questioning: Clarifying the Concept

- Why are you saying that?
- What exactly does this mean?
- How does this relate to what we have been talking about?
- What do we already know about this?
- Can you give me an example?

The Dying Gaul – Epigonus (230 BC)

The Dying Gaul is a landmark in western art and culture because it is the first instance showing an enemy of Greece (the word 'Gaul' was adopted only recently) as brave, human and sensitive. The Greeks had a long standing hegemonic world view in which they were superior in every way to barbarians (unshaven, babbling people beyond the Hellenic sphere). Thus this statue demonstrates a level of compassion, realism and respect not yet seen before.

This sculpture was made in Roman times and is based on the lost Greek original.

Great Debates

Yes, there are no savage and civilized peoples.

- The image of savage people is related to their level of technological sophistication. If I have a servant boil some tea for me and bring it to the drawing room, I am not more civilized than someone in New Guinea who is boiling some roots for himself next to his straw hut. He would be pleased to have someone pour his tea in a silver teapot too.

^ from pacatrue.blogspot.com

- Primitive or 'savage' cultures have been deprived of education so they are not to blame – in fact we are to blame. So-called modern societies display equally savage behaviour if you look for it. Recent Western history has a lot of human rights abuses. If something is right or wrong for others, it is right or wrong for us too. We need to stop being hypocrites otherwise no one can take us seriously. People always think their culture is superior. The view that someone is savage is just a lack of understanding / bigotry / chauvinism. They don't see that the Holocaust, racism, Stalinism, apartheid, slavery, genocide, unjust wars all happened in civilized societies.

- Savage peoples are correctly adapted for their own environment. Western values do not apply everywhere. Having several wives makes sense among herders, not among hunters. Evolution means that 'good / bad' behaviour has developed in individuals as a survival strategy in a particular group. The behaviour of one culture is perfectly adapted to suit their environment. No society has an 'anything goes' approach to morals. Everyone in the world has moral standards. We just don't understand other cultures well enough.

^ adapted from Clyde Kluckhohn, *Mirror for Man*

- There are no truly civilized cultures in this world. A truly civilized culture would not fight in wars, even when attacked and would not need laws. Its people would not hurt each other. If you look at the terrible things that so-called civilized cultures do to themselves and the rest of the world, then a so-called savage society is a welcome relief. At least they are connected to nature. 'Savage' peoples and societies are healthier.

- Who sets the standard for progress? We do and that makes us biased. Our system is no better than any other's. We have junk food, over-medication, waste of resources, obesity, crime, alcoholism, wild youths and many other social ills. What makes us so special? The amount of money in our pockets? I don't think so – what about our moral corruption? We are the savages.

- Let's not generalize and say all these people are this and we are all this. The fact is, in the world, *people are people*. As individuals and as cultures we have more in common with each other than what separates us. Let's study similarities not differences. Generalizations are lazy ways of thinking – putting people in boxes and labeling how they behave. This does not stand up to scientific study. There is only one race – the human race and we should not forget the importance of this. The man is the measure of all things, not the culture.

No, some cultures are more civilized than others.

- It is possible for a people to become corrupted for a time. Nazi Germany or Imperial Japan might be an example of a savage people. Some people think that the Muslims are a backward culture stuck in the past, and blame them for many of the world's problems. There are plenty of savage peoples. Do we really need to go down the list? The fact is that all humanity is savage. You'd have to be blind, deaf, and dead not to see it. If we pretend that there is no right or wrong, then shall we just ignore things like massacres and war crimes?

^ Iconoclast421 — anythingexceptthetruth.blogspot.com

- If someone is living in a rainforest and their trees get cut down and the land is used for farming, that's just bad luck. This is progress and if jungle people are not adaptable, they lose. Law of the jungle, survival of the fittest. Why should I care about them? This is human progress and economic development. If people cannot live in the normal world of TVs, cars, houses and jobs, it's their fault.

- Cultural relativism does not equal moral relativism. Moral relativism means there are no universal moral standards in the world — which is not actually true. There is, however, a universal *lack* of standards, which is more pronounced in some cultures than in others. In the past people thought slavery was good. If we take the view that no culture is uncivilized then we would still have slavery today and no women would have the vote either. Someone needs to show us our faults so we can progress as a society.

- Some things are plainly savage no matter how you look at them: cannibalism, suttees, human sacrifice, and slavery. It is right that these and other human rights violations have been stopped and this should continue. Some civilizations are more evolved than other cultures in the world. Some cultures have developed further and discovered more. The rest of the world needs to learn from these and see the West as the peak of human achievement.

- Primitive cultures lack education, resources and infrastructure compared to modern countries. Plus their food is often terrible so they are not strong and healthy and they often die young. This makes them 'savage' and they have a long way to come to meet the standards of truly civilized societies. This is a burden for the rich countries. Modern rich countries have a responsibility to teach them. What is right or wrong for one group, is right or wrong for others too.

- Let's not romanticize primitive societies. They are what they are; basic and undernourished, under-educated and generally not well off. They cannot put a man on the moon nor can they always judge the difference between right and wrong. Primitive peoples, like children, need guidance and education to help them achieve independence and stability. Let's not be weak and ignorant about this.

The Blue-Eyed, Brown-Eyed Game

This famous game was developed by Jane Elliot and is very effective and easy to enact. But it can be controversial so you may want to discuss the history and use of it. Otherwise to play it, you need to keep the students in the dark as to the point of the exercise. First split the class into two groups based on something to do with their origins. Originally it was eye colour. Then you grant one group exceptional privileges over the others; giving them longer breaks, more encouragement and allow them to taunt the others.

With the other students, a band around their necks is placed on each of them by members of the superior group. You tell the inferior group that they are below the others, they are not as good or as smart and must do what they are told. They must sit at the back of the class and they are given generally short shrift by the teacher. And so it goes on. There is a lot of psychological manipulation involved but once you have gone far enough with it and the inferior group are thoroughly fed up with their situation, then you turn the tables.

Once this happens, there is a realization that the game and the precept behind it is not a fun or nice one and that it's extremely unfair. When this occurs you can allow the class to equalize and mingle again – which they do eagerly. This moral exercise is especially useful in teaching children about racism and diversity. For adults in companies it encourages them to be more team-oriented and to not look down on juniors and the more menial staff lower down the organization.

Vocab Refresh

Savage – cruel, furious, animal-like, wild.

Sophisticated – refined, polished, polite, knowledgeable.

New Guinea – an isolated Asian country which has the highest diversity of languages in the world.

Bigotry – intolerance and possibly hatred of a group of people based on their beliefs.

Chauvinism – a feeling of unwavering superiority towards a group of people. Belittling people.

The Holocaust – the genocide of 6 million Jews during World Wart II.

Apartheid – the old policy of racial prejudice, discrimination and segregation in South Africa.

Obesity – being very fat.

Cultural relativism – the view that cultures cannot be judged against any single standard culture.

Moral relativism – the view that morals are not constant across all peoples.

Cannibalism – the practice of eating people. This is still rumoured to occur in remote parts of the New Guinea highlands.

Suttees – an outlawed Indian custom where the widow of a deceased man would throw herself on his funeral pyre.

Undernourished – underfed, lacking nutrition.

Primitive – basic.

Ignorant – lacking in knowledge or refusing to acknowledge a proven fact. Being unenlightened.

Survival – the quality of being able to live through challenging circumstances.

Adapted – suited to one's environment.

The End